Raven

Raven

Hiking 1,000 Miles on the Appalachian Trail with Double Vision

Lisa Cohen

For my tramily.
Thank you for the journey.

CONTENTS

ACKNOWLEDGMENTS

Raven would not have been possible without the support from various sponsors and contributors. Thank you to Eberhard Gobel, Sawyer, Mariani, Flatout, Hudson Valley Hikers, Caysey Herschaft, Steven Yansick, Lisa Parker, Lori Beer, Megumi Splash, Tim Kinetic, Alexander Turoff, Barley Hyde, William Sarokin, Douglas Meyer, Chris DiBona, Jim Edson, Gary McGraw, Andrew Reynolds, Michele Zaretsky, Jason Frankel, Richard Brideau, The Cohens, The Ro Family, and all my anonymous supporters...my trail angels.

Chapter 1: 45.9044° N, 68.9216° W

The first hike I can remember was in grade school, my classmates and I walked miles across fields, climbed over a fence stile and had lunch among the leaves on the Appalachian Trail. The first hike I was simply, Lisa.

Years after grade school when I was twenty-six I decided to take my first long hike. Before I left for the start of the Appalachian Trail I considered a trail name to carry over the miles instead of Lisa, I would be called Raven. Trail names can be symbolic, humorous or created as short references for true and long-distance hikers.

Traditionally fellow hikers give or don trail names to one another based off personality and circumstance. A hiker who is always early to wake up and start hiking might be called Early Riser. Another hiker who always borrows or asks for food might be called Yogi. In my case, Raven was a name given to me during my undergraduate years as a college DJ. As Raven I hosted a radio jazz hour, dressed as the comic book character for conventions and found an attraction for Fjallraven apparel. In Swedish fjallraven translates into Artic fox, which I felt fitted my personality, I wore the symbol on my winter hat and along the edges of the trekking pants I hemmed for hiking (I was and will always be short).

I was Raven when I introduced myself along the trail and although a few other trail names were tempted on me, they never stayed. I was called The Quietest Girl from New York, Mary Poppins, The Last Avenger and Slippy, but nothing connected with me as strong as Raven. I walked over a thousand miles carrying my trail name and I was lucky to never meet another Raven along the trail to compete with. My tramily, trail family, and I were always looking out for other hikers with similar names and we did for a while, find hikers from the past with their names written on the shelter walls. During a long stretch around Virginia it seemed we were following in the footsteps of a previous thru hiker named Nomad. Nomad, the one I hiked with, wasn't always Nomad though.

The very first night of my hike when I reached Springer Mountain in Georgia I walked up to the shelter and asked if there was room for one more. I met a ridge runner; a few hikers with no trail names yet, JW and a man who passed around drinks. Because of the drinks, Nomad was originally given the trail name of Bourbon. Trail names like Bourbon and The Quietest Girl from NY are not always ideal, often given by other hikers; the suggestions don't always match the person they are or want to be while on the hike. At times trail names can be literal, JW was named for being a Jehovah's Witness and he wore the name as I did my own, on his hat and also on his hiking shirt. We also knew of another literal hiker named 82 who was named because his pack weighed a total off 82 pounds.

A well-known hiker named Tear Drop had another precise trail name, titled after a tear shaped tattoo was inked onto his face. Pace was named for the consistent pace she kept while hiking. Wasabi was named because she was usually found sitting at the shelter, eating spicy wasabi peas. Quest was on a quest (he ended up building his own raft and aqua blazing down a river). Rebel, he was on his second thru hike attempt and was rebellious. Fed ex flashed a fed ex truck, Lightweight carried an ultra light Z Packs backpacking pack. Teach often passed on teacher wisdom, how to tie our hiking shoes efficiently or wrap around bear bag rope. Lemsip was named after a cold remedy in England and her hiking partner, also from England; Rictic was based off a record label. Fedora the Explorer was never seen, even while hiking, without his classic fedora on his head. Gourmet had professionally prepared dehydrated food in every mail drop that his mother sent to him. Tea Time was the combination of a couples trail name, who always traveled with tea in their food bags, individually they were called Tin Cup and Hot Tea.

Tea, or more specifically, sweet tea is well known in the south and along the southern sections of the Appalachian Trail. As "The Quietest Girl from New York" I had to learn that tea was everywhere on the trail and especially sweet tea in every trail town below the Mason Dixon Line. In Gainesville while ordering my first southern sweet tea I met one of my first trail angels down in Georgia.

Trail angels are people who hikers meet along the trail or in trail towns that help out, whether offering a ride, a place to stay or in the thoughtfulness of sharing food. Trail angels are known generously around the southern states for setting up tables of food for hikers or providing water at parking lots and sections where the trail crosses a road. When a trail angel helps out a hiker, even if they are not there and simply leave soda or fruit in a box, hikers call this trail magic. In the beginning of a long distance hike, trail magic can help provide encouragement and the energy to keep a hiker going. Georgia, during my hike, had the greatest trail magic, which eased my daily miles and moral. I met Cedar Tree near The Benton MacKaye Trail who gave me his own rain gear Packa, was saved with a hitch into town at Unicoi Gap after falling down Blue Mountain and I had the greatest experience at Dicks Creek Gap from Greeter, Bigfoot and Ms. Bigfoot. Greeter and his friends had table upon table laden with food for hikers, comfortable chairs for us to rest on and kind words of encouragement. Trail magic can be elaborate or even as simple as a bag of apples left underneath a tree.

The very first trail magic I received was back in New York on the Appalachian Trail along Bear Mountain. Before I left for Georgia, my father organized a send off hike with the group we belonged called Hudson Valley Hikers. Although it was winter with the ground still covered in snow, fifty hikers showed up to wish me luck and join a hike before I headed south. Together we walked around the zoo, across the Bear Mountain Bridge and followed the blue blazes up Anthony's Nose. At the end of the day while everyone said goodbye another hiker named Lisa held out her hand and gave me a bracelet for good luck. I wore that bracelet as I hiked every mile on the trail until I reached the coordinates, which it displayed, for the last blaze on the Appalachian Trail, the summit of Mount Katahdin in Maine.

The last trail magic I received was at Baxter State Park at the base of the last trail mountain in Maine. Still wearing my bracelet I stuck out my hand and hitched a ride for Nomad and I to travel into the nearby town of Millinocket. We were lucky with no cell service or rangers in the wooded area we managed to find a trail angel on his way out of the park who offered to drive us all the way to the Appalachian Trail Café in town. A ride into town after hiking for sixteen solid hours sounded like magic to our ears. It was magic alone to simply meet a man who before noon had summit Mount Katahdin, spent years hiking The Greats, hiked Mt. Marcy the highest peak in New York and even conquered Everest.

Chapter 2: Double Vision

I never thought about Everest, but for years I dreamed about the Appalachian Trail. I was raised from the mountains, where I learned to explore fire towers, rock climb, snowshoe up hills and fall asleep under the trees. When I started to dream about hiking the trail from Georgia to Maine, I didn't have double vision. I was an undergraduate student studying poetry and minoring in wilderness education, learning how to hold an ice pick properly and receiving grades for throwing bear bag ropes into the air perfectly.

In my college intro to backpacking course the students learned why a bear bag is necessary for hiking overnight in the woods. A bear bag carries and protects food from the animals in the mountains, even from the numerous shelter mice. At night after we cooked dinner from our portable stoves my classmates and I would walk over to a tree and with rope, throw the line over a high tree branch. After securing the food bag on the line we would hoist the bag into the air and tie the rope around the base or a lower limb of the tree, for retrieval in the morning.

Although I spent hours in my course practicing, I don't have the aim anymore that I used to. I can no longer find the branch on my first try, or even the second. I see two of everything. In my view there are two trees, two ropes, and double of every branch that I need to see. When I hold a bear bag rope in my hands and aim for a tree branch, I blink one eye closed; I try to remember what it felt like to have accurate depth perception. I sometimes remember how easy it once was, to see.

When I was twenty three and starting graduate school, I started to realize there were days I was too dizzy, too unbalanced to walk to class. I tried to tell myself it was nothing and to wait for the feeling to go away, but I never felt better. On a break from courses I drove hours home to visit family who suggested I have everything checked out. It began with a visit to an ear, nose and throat doctor. The doctor tested hearing, reactions and my sight. I sat in a dark room while my eyes followed lights moving on a screen, at the end warm and then cold air was blown into my ears. The ENT explained that my results seemed normal, but he would order a MRI for precautionary measure. I never had a MRI before or knew anyone who had, for safe measure I requested an open MRI machine.

An open machine allowed for my father to sit in the room with me, he waited by the door reading to me from a book. I welcomed the distraction, although it was hard to hear the words, the story eased my anxiety after a nurse took a needle to my arm injecting contrast solution for the scan. After the test was complete, we bookmarked the novels page and waited in the lobby for the okay to leave. My father and I waited for a long while until the nurse apologized for the delay; she explained that the computers were running slowly, but they weren't.

The morning after my brain scan I was heading out the door to drive upstate to my apartment and return for graduate school. I was making plans to avoid the traffic and find the best route when I received the call. The MRI found a mass about 2.7cm on the cerebellum, the balance center, of my brain.

After speaking with the ENT he recommended a neurologist who set up an appointment, as soon as possible. In the exam room he shone a light into my eyes, watched as I walked around the room and observed my balance in the hallway. The doctor measured every reaction time and asked all the routine questions before inviting my family and I into his office. The doctor let us know I had no dangerous symptoms; I tested to have normal vision, hearing and balance. Although everything appeared normal, the mass was possibly growing and pushing in on the brain, causing recent headaches and fatigue. The mass had probably been there for years, because of the location the doctors recommendation was removal and soon.

After thanking the neurologist we went back to my family's house and pretended to sip tea in the living room. We sat together silently around the couch, my parents didn't know what to say and I didn't either. I thought I had to return to college and the way things were. My break at home was ending; I had bills to pay, a studio apartment waiting, djing on campus and four graduate courses with upcoming papers to write. I couldn't think about brain surgery, I had a life I had to return to, and I tried. I drove what felt like the longest ride of my life, alone and anxious back to my upstate apartment. When I arrived I cleaned, cooked meals and when it was time for class I went. I wasn't there though, I sat in my desk while the class analyzed a discussion novel, but all I heard in my head were the words *brain surgery*. Before the first hour passed, I excused myself to the restrooms, walked out of the classroom into the closest stairwell I could find and I cried.

I had more MRI's to schedule, hospitals, neurosurgeons, and surgery on the closing in horizon. I loved the upstate apartment, it's independence and my studies, but I couldn't handle everything hundreds of miles away from family. I needed a new plan. I met with each of the graduate school professors and told them my story, asking for any possibility to complete the college semester. We found an answer; I would move back home and finish courses online, taking additional make up exams and attending classes virtually on a web camera. I thanked everyone repeatedly, went back to my apartment and began packing.

I packed my dining room table, two chairs, one mirror, clothes, an ottoman and dishware all tightly together into my small car. I wrote an ad online for everything else "free for pickup" I left behind my desk, television stand, bed frame and mattress. I also left behind the first place that had ever been just my own. My home.

After returning downstate, I started catching up on online assignments, attending courses virtually and looking for a neurosurgeon. The first neurosurgeon ordered another series of MRI's to see if and where the mass spread. During my second MRI, I was placed in a closed machine and felt panicked when asked to lay my head completely flat and still. I couldn't do it. The technicians kept leaning me back, until frustrated giving up and suggesting I order another MRI, this time under sedation. For my third MRI I arrived early in the morning at an image scan facility where I had the complete package, full under sedation. I woke up and the scans were done, but they weren't done correctly. After a call from the neurologist I learned I had to go in for a fourth MRI, where I was again put under sedation until the scans were finally complete.

I brought my test results to a neurosurgeon who explained the mass had not spread past the cerebellum and the mass was called a brain tumor. We scheduled the date for the end of May, after I finished finals and completed my semester of online courses I would go in for brain surgery.

The operation was set. The surgery would take a few hours, I was told there would be no pain and I would be fine. I packed a suitcase of books and clothes while spending my time worrying over how many socks I should bring. I tried not to think about the surgery, focusing on my final essays along with literary analysis papers about Dr. Seuss and social protest. I was busy with college and when I had time to be curious for medical answers, my surgeon warned not to research anything. He thought there was too much negativity online, along with possible worse case scenarios. I couldn't worry over what I didn't know would happen.

One morning in May at a hospital in Connecticut I went in for brain surgery. The team of doctors and the surgeon completely removed the tumor. I spent nine days in the hospital recovering.

When I woke from surgery I could barely see, my world was entirely distorted and blurry. Instead of one, everything in the hospital room was doubled and I struggled to distinguish my family from the faces of the doctors. I met countless nurses and physical therapists, which I could never recognize or acknowledge if seeing. Every day I tried to open my eyes and strain to improve, but my vision wasn't the only problem.

Because the surgery was on my brain and the cerebellum, I lost the ability to accurately send messages from the brain to my body. I couldn't convince my eyes to work together or any part of my left side to work correctly. When I woke up the first thing I noticed were my eyes, but I learned I had to struggle also with walking using my left leg, my left hand and even breathe enough from my left side to communicate. My brain tumor was removed and I was lucky because it wasn't life threatening, but the moment air reaches the brain, the damage is done. I was left to recover indefinitely.

The neurosurgeon checked on me with the results before I left the hospital, the tumor was benign and considered a pilocytic astrocytoma. My tumor was a type typically found in young children and judging by the size he assumed I had the tumor growing inside me for ten years. It wasn't wonderful to hear the good news; I didn't feel lucky or blessed that I was leaving the hospital in a wheelchair.

For a month I could not walk, I spent twenty-three hours a day in a bed sleeping and dreaming. When the physical therapist arrived my family helped me to a walker and I would attempt to make a path around the house. I couldn't connect my brain and the body; I couldn't move my left leg in step with the right. I couldn't pick up a fork with my left hand; I could barely see the fork. I couldn't watch television or movies, or imagine picking up a book to read from. For a month I was a vegetable. My mother washed my hair and tried every morning to feed me oatmeal and blueberries. By the time I was suppose to have gone back to graduate school, I was living in an inpatient rehabilitation hospital and I weighed only eighty-eight pounds.

In the inpatient hospital I lived in a stroke ward, because the brain injury floor was considered too busy. I woke up every morning to nurses taking samples of my blood, aids helping me walk to the bathroom and being watched as I washed my hair in the shower. All day long I went to physical, occupational and speech therapy sessions, twice. I learned how to walk safely, hold objects again in my hand, breathe well enough for full sentences and strengthen my eyes. I learned to eat again, no hiker hunger comparisons, but I could cook food despite my ongoing fear of knives.

When I wasn't working in the therapy kitchen or out in the therapy gym, I was walking the hospital hallways trying to keep my gait in a straight and "normal" line. I went to vocational therapy where I tried to meditate in a circle with the other patients. We closed our eyes and the incense brought us to the beach and although I tried to imagine, I could never walk well enough to withstand falling in the sand. In the evenings I practiced balancing on one foot, staring at hart charts I taped to the walls of my hospital bedroom. When I was tired I sat by the window looking out at the mountains. After a few weeks living at the hospital my insurance ran up and it was time to go home.

After my release I spent months in physical, occupational, speech, vestibular and vision therapy, continuing to challenge myself. In time, I was able to read novels again, sing along with Meatloaf on the record player and walk to the local grocery store while only falling once or twice. After taking a year away from college I transferred to a closer school, reapplied as a nonfiction major and set my aim on finishing my degree. I returned to graduate school in the fall and gained strength in the classroom and out, after a few months I realized I had the confidence to hike again. While navigating the sidewalks with double vision and ataxia, I knew I could walk the trails in town and eventually at home again in the mountains.

Sometimes when I'm on the trail or in the mountains I struggle. Since my surgery, I still have double vision, where I see two of every object in front of me, no matter the angle or viewpoint. Sometimes I close one eye for accuracy, but then I lose half of the view and I lose the ability to have depth perception. After the surgery I developed nystagmus in my left eye and now it appears to be slight in my right as well. Nystagmus is a condition where the eye is constantly jumping or in my case, pivoting like a broken clock hand. I see double but in the left eye the object is moving. My jump is slight and unnoticeable to other people, but very noticeable to me, especially when reading and the letters move on the page. In addition to the eyes, I have tinnitus in my left ear; it is a never-ending ring that I can sometimes choose to ignore. I learned I cannot hear the ticking of a watch, light rain or quiet noises if they're coming from my left side. Light noises I enjoy, I have headaches almost every day, but they are easier to live with when I am outside and hiking. I have sensitivity to noise and light, for months after my surgery I wore sunglasses daily, I adjusted with practice.

I adjust and still try to improve the ataxia on the left side of my body. After the surgery doctors took a camera down to see my vocal cords quiver. I don't breathe correctly on the left side and have trouble hiking and talking, or even just in talking long sentences out loud. I have ataxia in my left hand, it is slow and although I can hold a trekking pole, my grip is not strong. I have ataxia in my left leg, I cannot stand on one foot, balance or run, but I can walk.

I walk, move and see differently, but I can challenge myself. I read a book once about a man who was blind, he decided he wanted to hike the Appalachian Trail and he did. In his footsteps, I realized I could follow.

I had brain surgery, past tense, but I will always have a brain injury. My injury challenges me to see, move and to live in each and every moment. Although my brain injury is invisible, I don't have a broken leg or wear a cast, I struggle and refuse to let my body keep me from my goals. Before my surgery I only dreamed about hiking long distances, I admired the trail, but I was missing the motivation. Surgery changed me; it helped me take one shaky step closer to the two million I would take on the Appalachian Trail.

Chapter 3: Georgia
79 Official Trail Miles

The traditional route of a hiker traveling on the Appalachian Trail is a northbound route starting at Springer Mountain in Georgia. Backpacking starting in the south and ending in Maine is encouraged for following the weather and traveling along with the bubble of hikers. Because I hiked often, but never backpacked alone, I set my sights on a northbound route starting with the crowd of hikers in March. Before I left to join the bubble for Georgia, I lived and trained for hiking in the trail town of Wingdale New York.

Wingdale is small with a nearby post office, one motel, a pizza place or two and the Metro North Railroad. I moved to Wingdale to live near the train, because I have double vision, I sold my car and relied on the railroad and preferred my feet for travel. When I wanted to hike I would walk three miles from my house on the road to reach the white markers of the trail. I trained weekly adjusting my pack weight in northbound and southbound hikes heading from the Appalachian Trail Rail Road Station. After months of training I booked a ticket and planned the beginning of my journey down to the hiker hostel in Georgia and the start of the A.T.

Because I'm not a fan of flying or the airports, I reserved a seat on an Amtrak train for a seventeen-hour trip south to Gainsville Georgia. In the winter I had one last shakedown hike, repacked my backpacking bag and headed to the Amtrak in Penn Station New York City. Carrying a full backpacking pack on the train, into Grand Central and around the city was an experience. With time to spare in Bryant Park I stopped at the benches for a short trail lunch of animal crackers and dried fruit. It felt completely strange to be starting my trip by leaving such a busy place for the mountain wilderness. I had a nice send off from my family and then a classic New York City experience by an attempted panhandler in the station terminals. After the woman tried to shake me down for cash, I was ready to leave the north behind. When boarding was called I walked to the train and looked for a seat by the window. Sitting with my pack at my feet I opened up a book and began to read, the pages passed and the train covered the miles in hours, what would take me months to walk.

In stark comparison to the city I woke up in the southern countryside to realize that I was the only passenger disembarking in Gainesville Georgia. I fell asleep hours earlier with my feet resting on my pack, to the voice of the southern woman besides me; her accent was new and comforting. In a similar southern accent, the conductor called me to the train door and I placed my pack on my shoulders stepping down from the makeshift staircase he placed onto the dirt ground, my first steps in Georgia. I looked around at the empty station and placed a call to the hostel shuttle driver who agreed earlier for a ride. Unluckily my train was delayed earlier in Baltimore Maryland and the driver suggested I wait in a nearby café until he could reach me in town.

I walked around the town briefly until I found the café and without thinking I opened the door. (I didn't yet know hiker etiquette; backpackers traditionally leave their packs outside before entering an establishment). I looked over the room and nervously sat down at the counter on a tall stool, placing my pack next to my feet, where it immediately fell over laying sideways on the floor. I attempted to appear well skilled opening my pack to take out my guidebook and readjusting it's position to stand straight. I was looking over the miles from the approach trail to Springer Mountain when a generous man on the other side of the counter offered a southern breakfast, biscuits and gravy with sweet tea.

An hour later the driver from the hiker hostel arrived and we headed over to the hostel in Dahlonega. The hiker hostel was gorgeous, I walked around the trails outside several times, while the hostel's dog followed running circles around the path. I met a few hikers who were already hiking the trail and a few like me, who were about to start. In the morning everyone woke early for a homemade breakfast of pancakes and coffee. I was too nervous too eat, but I sat around at a table with my book and sipped slowly at a glass of orange juice. After breakfast we gathered our packs into the hostel's vans and headed out for Springer Mountain.

The Appalachian Trail officially begins at the first white blaze on top Springer, but there are a few hikers who choose to start at the approach trail and climb the mountain following blue blazes. The majority of the hikers leaving from the hostel chose to start the trail at the mountain's summit, including a man I met named Fedora. Before we headed out everyone said good luck and then I was in a shuttle headed to the approach trail 8.8 unaccounted for miles that are not a part of the A.T. I felt if I was going to start my journey it would be by climbing the mountain, and to follow the great hiker advice and remember to *hike your own hike*. As the shuttle pulled away I walked into the building at the foot of the mountain to register. I waited in line until I was given the number 303. I was the 303 attempted thru hiker of the class of 2017. Back outside I stood under the famous archway as everyone took pictures of the beginning. Five of us hikers were starting from the approach trail; I smiled wearing my green bandana holding onto my pack under the arch.

It was a warm day; I left the archway and headed to the path on the left following the approach trail and the strenuous steps to Amicalola Falls. I paused at the sign to pull my hair up and give a smile to the couple behind me, Lemsip and Ric Tic from Britain. We hiked our first steps north, pausing on every ledge along the stairs for a chance to catch our breath. There were no white blazes, but there we were, standing at the top of the falls and realizing there were miles and miles left before reaching the summit of Springer Mountain and our glimpse at the first white blaze.

For hours a group of us trailed along together, we talked about mushrooms and edible plants until I decided to stop on my own for lunch. I found a tree log along the trail to sit down on and waved goodbye to the other hikers, not knowing if we would ever meet again. I stared for several minutes at my lunch of trail mix, but I wasn't really hungry. I passed the time readjusting my packs shoulder straps until I looked up at the cloudy sky; I thought about rain and attached my trekking umbrella before heading further up the mountain.

On the way to the summit I introduced myself to a few hikers, most of who passed me while heading up inclines. In the afternoon I passed one hiker myself, named Jaybelle, another solo female, who I learned was from Queens New York. I lost my sunglasses, backtracked and still my pace was enough to pass her again, twice. Confession, I did not lose my sunglasses. I was alone on the trail and could not find the next blue blaze to follow, I turned around backtracked unnecessarily and then resumed hiking northbound following another hiker who appeared to see the blazes with no doubt. Jaybelle had a steady pace, but after passing her twice I spent a few moments to slow down and walk with her, worrying if she would make it to a shelter or find a tent spot before the rain and an incoming storm.

The approach trail felt like one of the longest hikes I had ever taken, with every incline I wondered how much further. I told Jaybelle encouragingly that it couldn't be much longer, but of course it was. With the rain beating down I quickened my pace, said goodbye to Jaybelle and hiked on alone. (Jaybelle ended up staying the night at the shelter on the approach trail, a mile and a half short of the summit and safe away from the storm). It continued to rain on and off while I climbed the hills and I met a few other thru hikers. A girl taller, but younger then me named Wasabi stopped at my sight while I struggled adjusting my trekking umbrella and we laughed.

At the summit I met a young man who seemed in a hurry to cover additional miles, we enjoyed the view together and he said good luck before heading out. After he left I had a few minutes alone with the trail register, the sign and my first white blaze of the trail. I had done it I hiked Springer Mountain; I was hiking the Appalachian Trail. I opened the trail logbook behind the rock and wrote my first trail entry "March 1, 2017: March First a new month, the beginning of my hike and Brain Injury Awareness Month". Although I had a brain injury and I hiked the approach trail with double vision, nothing was stopping me. I looked down on the mountain and from my eyes I saw two of the first white blaze, a double image that was mine and mine alone, and it was beautiful.

I smiled, put the logbook back in the rock and headed down the trail to Springer Mountain Shelter, just as the thunder began. I passed a large grouping of tents and found the shelter, since it was late and near sundown I was the last one to ask for room and I luckily found a nice spot upstairs next to the female ridge runner. I set my pack down on the floor and spent time with everyone watching the hikers cook their food as I slowly nibbled on animal crackers. After dinner I realized I was running low on water and walked over to filter from a nearby stream. The sun went down and the rain was coming down hard, I

switched into camp sandals and immediately my feet
fell into several muddy puddles. Day one and dirty feet.

After gathering water I went to hang my bear bag
and learned the site had cables near the shelter. I was
custom to hanging bear bags, I never saw bear cables
before. Staring up tentatively I shook my head and then
walked back over to the shelter, I asked for help. I was
thankful the ridge runner was patient and showed me
how to clip on and hoist up my food bag high enough
to be out of a bears reach. With my stove less dinner
and chores done, I went to sleep early upstairs
alongside the ridge runner and another hiker, who
would later be named Nomad. Every hour until
morning we were woken by the sounds of thunder
along with the window of the shelter banging open and
close long in the night.

In the morning I woke up slowly and found almost
every other hiker already left the shelter. I put on socks
over muddy feet, shoes, gaiters, shoved my sleeping
bag, rolled my sleeping pad away and talked with
Nomad before he left. *How could anyone sleep through that
storm and had I noticed the mice?* I had a short breakfast,
realized my poptart pastry was frozen beyond hope of
consumption and headed out as the last hiker down
from the mountain. The weather was cold and I found
the trail was icy in several spots, I warned the hikers
heading up to be careful not to slip. When I descended
the mountain the trail walked by a parking lot (for
hikers skipping the approach trail) where I nodded to
the ridge runner looking over and assessing a new
group of hikers.

In the afternoon I caught up with a few other hikers and I was walking with Nomad near the Benton MacKaye trail when we met a hiker named Cedar Tree, the inventor of the Packa. Cedar Tree took one look at my trekking umbrella that I was using as my rain gear and he took out his very own Packa and handed it to me, trail magic. The Packa in the rain covered me, my pack and would become my favorite piece of gear. I thanked Cedar Tree and waved goodbye as we parted ways; I realized how a moment chance meeting could change everything.

I hiked alone in the evening after stopping for food and to filter water before ending for the day at Hawk Mountain Shelter. The first day I hiked nine miles and day two was 8.1 since the shelter was .2 miles west from the trail. In my pack I carried an ultra light tent, but from the beginning I preferred setting up at shelters instead of camping tent spots. I walked up to the shelter and introduced myself to a male ridge runner, a young hiker named Rebel and said hello to JW, Wasabi, Pace, Nomad, LadyBug and her father Flashdaddy. Everyone laughed as Rebel kept us entertained all night; he previously attempted a thru hike of the Appalachian Trail and had countless stories. Near sundown when I went to bear cable my food bag I overheard JW mention that I was the quietest New Yorker he ever met. To complete my quiet girl persona, I fell asleep early while everyone else planned on meeting up the next night, putting in our longest mileage yet, 12.5 trail miles away at Woody Gap. The guidebook showed a real bathroom, garbage cans and a great tenting site that everyone thought was not worth missing.

I was last to head out in the morning again, finding my morning pack up routine to leave me behind the other hikers. I was starting out late, but I wanted to see if I could keep up with the miles and I planned my goal for the day to match the other hikers to Woody Gap. For the month of March, it was another cold morning, while climbing Sassafras Mountain I paused for awhile to catch my breath on the rocks. I was tired during the climb, feeling my pack weigh heavily on my shoulders and struggling to acclimate, I wanted to cry. Confession, I may have cried. I looked around feeling sorry for myself, removed my pack, took one deep breathe and then I realized how beautiful Georgia was. The southern plants and trees seemed greener than the trees in New York, which could have been from the absence of northern snow, but it was lovely. Truth be told I wouldn't have wanted to be anywhere else except for that mountain. I shouldered my pack and kept hiking until the rough incline was far behind me.

At a dirt road after Sassafras I ran into Rebel who dropped, lost or forgotten his smoking pipe (his token unnecessary thru hiker item) and he was walking around aimlessly searching for it. I believe it wasn't the first time he lost something while on the trail. I let him know I hadn't passed by anything on the trail and wished him luck in searching. I never saw Rebel again.

Towards the end of the day near a gap along a dirt road I met a day hiker who asked if I was indeed a thru hiker. He was surprised since I am short and on the small size, he told me he supposed I was only thirteen years old. When I insisted that I was indeed twenty-six with identification to prove it he offered me three cans of beer and his company. We walked together for the last hour of my day and when I told him my phone wasn't working he immediately handed me his cell phone. "When was the last time you called your ma?" He was right and upon dialing my mother sounded beyond grateful to hear the voice of her daughter hundreds of miles away. My mother is amazing and to hear her voice as I walked was encouraging, she was so happy I was hiking.

When I told my friends and family I was going to backpack the trail my ma, she stood up for me. I moved in with her a few years after my surgery, she knew my struggles, how far I went and would continue to go. I was grateful to know my family was back home in New York waiting and cheering me on. I thanked the day hiker, as did my mother, and he handed me chocolate, a gift from his wife, as we parted ways. Beer, chocolate and a phone call – he was simply amazing, a southern charm trail angel.

When I reached Woody Gap I looked around for minutes at the view of mountains, it was serene. The cascading ridges seemed to stretch for miles beyond the valley. It was comforting to see the mountains I climbed, as well as to see the restroom in front of me. As for a public restroom, it had no sink and the toilet did not flush, but it had a door and four walls to keep out the cold. I used the facilities, threw away my food wrappers in the solid bear proof garbage canister and enjoyed the lighter weight in my pack. Over in a field I looked around for everyone I knew from the night before, but the only people I recognized were LadyBug and Flashdaddy. I started to set up my tent within eyesight of theirs and realizing it looked pathetic they came over to help me readjust the pitch along with placing rocks down over the stakes to help offset the incoming wind. After thanking the two I ate my no cook dinner of cheese on crackers, shared the beer with a few hikers and threw my bear bag up into a distant tree. I missed the branch the first three times, but successful hung the bag of food after awhile and if I remember correctly, that was the only time I hung my own bear bag for the rest of the hike. I was lucky in the existence of bear cables, helpful hikers and in my tramily.

Just as the sun went down I walked over to the road to enjoy again the view, I looked across the way at a picnic bench along the hill and noticed a familiar hiker setting up his tent. I waved eagerly and went over to greet JW who arrived late at the gap; we sat together for a while looking over the sunset on the mountains. We relished knowing we hiked the long miles of the day when other hikers had not and made the distance to camp at Woody Gap.

The night before at Hawk Mountain Shelter as I fell asleep the group also agreed we would meet up at Neel Gap after Woody Gap to spend the night together at Blood Mountain Cabins. Neel Gap is the home to Mountain Crossings, an amazing outfitter and the location where most thru hikers quit to head home or abandon the trail. Hikers who are leaving mark their departure by throwing up their hiking boots into the branches of the trees surrounding the trail, which passes right under the building. JW, who became a trail father to us, called to book a cabin where we could all sleep warmly inside with the promise of a shower, laundry and pizza.

I dreamed about warm cooked pizza and woke up in the morning at Woody Gap freezing from the cold. I used my quick chilled pace to catch up to JW, who woke up earlier, and we started the long trek north to Neel Gap. Together we climbed Gladdis and then Blood Mountain, which was our steepest point yet on trail. At Blood Mountain I first started to feel like a real backpacker. On reaching the summit I threw down my pack and skipped over past the tourists to use the nearby privy. (Blood Mountain is part of the A.T and additionally a popular hike for clean smelling day hikers who seemed appalled that I expressed such joy to find a privy on top the mountain). I heard one woman, dressed fully in cotton with her partner carrying her pack for her exclaim, "Oh my gosh why would anyone in their right mind use a privy", it was apparently shameful and I was proud.

In comparison to the day hikers my friends and I were dressed in outdoor hiker gear and we hadn't bathed in days. The only routine I kept was dipping my bandana into passing frigid streams; we were not trying to impress anyone. Once I had my pack back on I met up with JW and two girls we were hiking alongside named Lumber Jill and Summer. We took pictures at the summit and headed slowly on the rocky descent from Blood Mountain towards Neel Gap.

Because the mountain was crowded with day hikers, there was a resemblance of an assembly line of people climbing down on the rocks. For an hour we followed behind a large family with a young boy who fell and then I too took a few slips. I was anxious about my hiking gait, how I appeared to walk with ataxia, so I encouraged JW to take the lead and hoped he didn't notice or hear my falls behind him. No matter the damage I knew I could always pick myself back up and keep walking north, my goal was to arrive at Mountain Crossings and buy an apple from the store along with a sweet tea. We talked about food for miles and how JW wanted nothing more then a cold soda when we reached the bottom.

By the afternoon we reached the store, left our packs outside and started shopping when we were reunited with Wasabi and Nomad. The two hitched a ride in, skipping Blood Mountain, not wanting to break their promise to meet us at the cabins. After asking for directions we walked over to our very own cabin. I was content, my apple was everything I dreamed it to be and the staff offered to do our laundry for us while we ordered pizza and played card games. The shower was also divine. While waiting for the laundry I put on my town dress and since it was cold I bought a souvenir shirt from the store to wear as a jacket. We spent the night in our town clothes watching movies, rearranging our gear and talking about food.

Before leaving New York in preparation for the

A.T I bought large amounts of my favorite hiking food for resupply. My mom was nice enough to agree to ship a box out to every town I wouldn't have time to shop for food in. One of my early oversights was the food I enjoyed while day hiking and weekend backpacking, was not the best for long term backpacking trips. After a few days on the trail I could no longer look at animal crackers, poptarts or any form of peanut butter on a cracker without regret. I would have to learn to make time and resupply in town grocery stores with wraps, cheese, jumbo iced honeybuns, dry fruit and my favorite mini m&m's. Before leaving Neel Gap when I opened my mail drop box I picked up, I gave away most of the food to Wasabi, Nomad and JW.

On our way back to the trail we stopped at Mountain Crossings for trail magic, hot dogs, chips and chocolate (as a vegetarian I ate two of the buns and kept the chocolate in my pocket for later). We were about to head out together when Nomad confessed his leg was hurting and he decided to take a zero day remaining behind at the cabins. We waved goodbye to Nomad, Lemsip and Rictic, who just arrived, and the three of us that remained headed up Levelland Mountain.

With the late start Wasabi, JW and I only hiked 6.7 miles before sundown to Whitley Gap Shelter. The Shelter was marked in our trail books as 1.2 miles off trail, but we were meeting Pace and as luck would have it right before the last mountain at Tesnatee Gap we had more trail magic. We met a man parked near a road with his truck grilling up burgers with an entire table laden down with trail snacks for us. I had a hamburger bun, grabbed a soda for later and a few bags of sour patch candy.

Our last mountain of the day was tiring, my pockets were weighed down with candy and soda, JW was feeling tired and we encouraged each other until finally reaching the shelter for the night. I enjoyed the day with my new tramily, but the constant conversation was difficult with my headaches and I needed a quiet place to myself for the night. While everyone set up their sleeping bags in the shelter I walked over to the nearby field and set up my tent alone overlooking a hill. The sun went down as I set in my last stake forming a somewhat working shelter that was slanted with just enough space to lie down in. After my setup I sat down with everyone at the picnic bench by the shelter, drank my soda before hanging my food bag up on the bear cables and wished everyone a goodnight. Alone in my tent site listening to the sound of lightly falling rain I blissfully fell asleep.

JW started out first in the shelter while I was still packing up my tent, he came over to let me know he was on his way. I finished packing up my gear, had food with Pace and Wasabi and then headed out while they were still finishing their breakfast. I spent the morning hiking up the hill and out from the 1.2 miles, which were still not counted as Appalachian Trail miles. I could hear J.W's voice in the back of my head laughing about the extra miles and not stopping the night before to cowboy camp on the rocks. I was glad to reach the official trail white blazes again and start towards wherever I wished to end hiking for the day.

I was walking along at a casual pace in the morning when I met a man slackpacking from Virginia. His wife was helping him slackpack, which meant he carried a lightweight daypack and met her at night, so as to not carry the full weight of a tent and sleeping bag. The man from Virginia was nice enough to slow his pace to hike with me; he taught me to remove the brain compartment from my bag to help lose pack weight. We ate lunch together and I enjoyed a banana that I saved from the trail magic, then we talked on and kept such a good pace that we passed two section hikers and JW.

At the end of the day after passing Chattahoochee Gap and the former site of Rocky Knob Shelter we reached Blue Mountain Shelter after hiking 13.3 miles. The campsite was crowded but I found a spot in the shelter to set up my sleeping pad and bag. After taking our packs off and settling in we sat with Pace, Wasabi, JW, along with a few other hikers around a traditional Georgia campfire. I passed around my animal crackers and after introducing myself to a few new faces told stories of my djing years and receiving the trail name Raven.

As the sunlight faded the girls and JW cooked their dinners and started to discuss their worry and plans about incoming rain. JW mentioned the possibility of taking his second zero day at the shelter (when I met him at Springer it was his first zero). A zero day is another hiker term, for when a hiker makes no mileage and stays in town enjoying food and warmth, or in some cases at shelters to avoid hiking in bad weather. Although it was a nice shelter on the mountain and the girl's idea of a trip into town for a zero day sounded interesting too, I fell asleep with my own plan to hike on despite the rain in the morning. I thought most seasoned backpackers walk on in the rain and I shouldn't let a storm keep me from adding on trail miles.

I woke up at Blue Mountain Shelter, rolled up my sleeping bag, took down my bear bag and headed out early attaching my trekking umbrella to my pack. A number of the remaining hikers looked curiously at my gear and one followed me out calling "Hey Marry Poppins"!

The trail down the mountain was hidden in mist and the sky rained as I headed slowly down the rocks. I could barely make out the white blazes on the trees and it was hard to keep an eye on the ground as well. On a steep slope I lost my balance on the wet rocks slipped and fell, for a while I couldn't get up. Alone I sat in the middle of the trail with rain streaking down my face and I thought I wasn't like everyone else. I couldn't walk or see correctly. I would fall on flat dry ground, why did I think I could backpack in the rain like everyone else?

I was in luck just when I was feeling down, I remembered the night before there was mention of a cooked breakfast trail magic at Unicoi Gap. I fell and it hurt, but I wasn't too far away from the gap. When I could move my leg, I stood up, brushed myself off and headed down to the nearest road with a parking lot.

It was the perfect morning trail magic; a camper with an overhang was set up cooking up omelets while a truck handed out fruit and juice boxes. The other hikers came and went while I dried off and decided to wait for Pace and Wasabi. The girls booked a night at a hotel in nearby Helen Georgia and when I asked they seemed happy to have me along. We stood waiting at the road for a hitch, until one of the trail magic men offered to give us a ride himself nine miles east and into town.

Once the last hiker came down from Blue Mountain we piled our equipment in his truck and were on our way to Helen. The girls and I were dropped off at the hotel after he showed us around with plans and a promise to meet later that night at Bigg Daddy's Tavern where he would buy us our first round of drinks. With our gear back at the hotel and a quick clean from the sink Wasabi, Pace and I walked around the town shops to the sound of German music. We hiked a nero day (near zero- low mile day) 2.4 miles to Unicoi Gap and we were glad to not be out on the mountain in the storm. We walked to a café where I bought a sweet tea and we sat outside under an umbrella looking out at the town.

In the afternoon Nomad hitched a ride into the village and together we all went to Bigg Daddy's for dinner. We shared stories on the walk to the restaurant and I explained why I wore glasses as a buffer for my eyes and double vision. Although the glasses didn't correct my vision, I felt they helped to hide the problem. The girls said they didn't notice, but l still wanted to continue hiding behind them, if just for a while longer.

At the restaurant I met BB and Magic Mic who started the same day on the trail and hiked with clippers agreeing to cut any hikers hair on the trail. Then to his word our trail magic man arrived and paid for everyone's first round of drinks. I had a Georgia Peach and it was perfect. I sat down next to Wasabi and ordered a portabella mushroom burger with fries, glad I was finally hungry for a nicely cooked meal.

After a few drinks the girls talked about life and confessed their worry about wanting to quit and leave the trail. Pace felt that in her eyes she had no moments where she felt right, that this was her journey. I hadn't said more then a few words all evening, but looked up from my burger long enough to share that these were the moments. So what if we weren't hiking in the rain? Having drinks and sharing the moments in town was a part of her, mine and all of our Appalachian Trail journeys. I turned over my wrist and revealed my tattoo and the bracelet I wore underneath it.

"When I think about the trail and quitting, even when I fall in the rain, I remind myself, this is where I've been and this is where I'm going."

On my wrist is a grey ribbon, a brain tumor awareness tattoo and below that the bracelet I was given back in New York as trail magic showing the coordinates to Mt. Katahdin, the northern terminus of the A.T.

Near sundown we finished our drinks and walked back to the hotel along the sidewalks of Helen Georgia.

I looked up at the cloudy sky and smiled knowing tomorrow I would be back to hiking the trail on the mountains underneath that same sky. I had fallen and left the trail for the day, but I was on my journey.

Chapter 4: Trail Romance

Cliché, until you realize your dating someone 24/7 in the woods, the relationship is real, raw and dirty. Literally, you meet someone and there is no time for dressing up, faking and putting your best foot forward. Your best foot hasn't been washed in four days, its covered in mud, calloused in miles and supporting the weight of you and your backpack. On the plus side you don't have to look nice for meeting the parents who would probably stare down at you nibbling on your animal crackers, hair unwashed and dirt surrounding you. The parents would probably smell you from outside their front door and wonder how in earth their child could put up with that smell.

Although I met Nomad the first night on the trail at Springer Mountain Shelter, we didn't hit it off until Helen Georgia. In the beginning I put hiking first, I introduced myself, but I was guarded. I slept upstairs in the shelter the first night in between the ridge runner and Nomad, but in the morning everyone headed out and I was alone. I met a few hikers and considered JW, Wasabi, Pace and Nomad friends, but for the first week while I was in Georgia I preferred hiking by myself.

While I was hiking by myself I fell on the trail and agreed on the ride into Helen Georgia with Pace and Wasabi. In Helen Nomad originally had plans to take a zero day with fellow hikers BB and Magic Mic, but on hearing my plans to return the next day he decided to head back to the trail with me instead. Wasabi and Pace wanted to skip ahead on the trail overpassing a few steep incline miles and that left just Nomad and I heading back to the mountain. Together we reorganized our packs in the hotel room before walking to the end of town in Helen and the local grocery store where we could resupply our food and catch a shuttle back to the trail. I walked slowly along the aisles while the song Tammy played overhead; I purchased dried kiwi and yogurt raisins to last for the next few days on trail. While we settled into the back of our ride, a pick up truck, the girls agreed that the four of us would meet again at the next trail town in Hiawassee Georgia and then later on in Franklin North Carolina for Pace's birthday.

Nomad and I hiked together the entire day from Unicoi Gap climbing up Rocky and Tray Mountain. He hiked slowly with my pace on the uphill and because his leg was hurting we were in step on the down hills. He told me how serendipitous he felt to meet me before revealing the tattoo on his arm. He explained how, as a teenager, he had a kidney transplant from his aunt. Years after the transplant his aunt died from a brain tumor.

We hiked until the afternoon sharing stories until we met another hiker heading north named Jeeves and learned of his stories. Jeeves could talk on the hills when I was too silent and felt winded; he fit into our pace perfectly. Nomad, Jeeves and I chose to end the day tenting at a mile marker known as Swag of the Blue Ridge. The boys set up their tents and started a fire; we sat around and shared stories while cooking dinner. Jeeves told us the story of the North Wind and the Sun.

"The Wind and the Sun had a bet,
The Wayfarer's cloak which should get;
Blew the Wind … the cloak clung;
Shone the Sun … the cloak flung
Showed the Sun had the best of it yet."

Near Hiawassee Georgia in the sun we sat sharing orange sodas when Nomad and I stopped for trail magic and a hitch into town for our first zero day together. We booked a night at The Budget Inn where we securely left our packs and headed into the village to meet JW, Wasabi and Pace at Daniels Buffet for dinner (the best mashed potatoes). Every hiker was sitting around the table dressed in brightly colored scrubs; they were staying at The Top of Georgia Hostel where the owners provided laundry and temporary clothing to borrow for hikers. We joked around, ate copious amounts of food from the buffet, and then went to the Mexican restaurant across the street for three-dollar margaritas. Before the night was over we toasted to our plans of all meeting again, after mile marker one hundred in North Carolina.

After everyone left the restaurant Nomad and I looked at the map and realized there was a movie theater a few miles down the road. We walked a few minutes, realized we would miss the movie at our pace, and then I stuck out my thumb and found us a hitch. Two girls pulled around and upon our invitation to join us at the movies, they laughed and said they had school the next day. We thanked them for the lift, purchased tickets and lounged out in the back of the theater to enjoy Logan the new Wolverine movie. It felt surreal to be in a southern movie theater wearing my town dress and hiker leggings sitting beside Nomad, a boy from Florida I only just met a week before. After the credits rolled we walked around the parking lot waiting for our taxi back to the inn and I thought about how happy I was to be in Georgia and the town of Hiawassee.

In the morning we went to Subway for breakfast and I watched longingly while Nomad ordered a warm freshly cooked bacon sub. On the trail I didn't have a stove or cooked food, I don't eat meat, I haven't for thirteen years, but it was still a meal to be admired. Our plan was made after breakfast, we checked out of the Budget Inn and into The Top of Georgia Hostel. We found two spots in the bunkroom where we hung our packs and donned our own scrubs to run around town wearing. We shared the room with two girls named Fed Ex and Lightweight and the group of us took a shuttle with an Amish brother and sister into town. Together with the girls we went back to Daniel's buffet (best macaroni and cheese ever) and walked around to the library where we sat out relaxing on the porch until finding our food resupply at Ingles Grocery. I had never been to an Ingles; I didn't know it was a popular grocery store down south. While shopping in the store wearing scrubs and arms full with nutella I realized I missed the trail.

Back at the hostel we met the hikers named Teardrop and Cuddles, who I met earlier without a trail name at the hiker hostel in Dahlonega. In the evening Lightweight and I cooked pizza in the hostel kitchen while comparing our love for the Harry Potter series.

After dinner, before we climbed into our bunks I remembered the Slackpacking Virginian's advice and removed the brain from my pack leaving it behind in the hiker box. I felt good, lighter and assure with my head on the pillow next to Nomad.

In the middle of the night I woke up to the surround sound splitting snores of the three people I was sharing a bunkroom with. I rolled over to cover my ears and immediately fell into the closet. The hostel bunk was up against the wall and had this ironically placed closet, which Nomad pulled me out of. Unable to disguise my laughter over the situation I calmed myself eating a bar of chocolate with orange until eventually I fell back asleep.

After weighing our packs outside the Top of Georgia hostel Nomad and I headed back to the trail with a worried Fed Ex and Lightweight. We were warned a snowstorm was coming in and Fed Ex wanted to leave the trail heading to the Florida Keys to wait it out on the beach. I had never been to Florida and smiled at the idea of a southern snowstorm. I learned to backpack in the Adirondacks of Upstate New York, walking across frozen lakes with heavy winter gear. I couldn't wait to see what the south had to offer. After the first incline the clouds came in and we passed the girls, wondering if we would ever see them again. We never did. Did they hike behind the snowstorm? Did they head back to the Florida Keys? We may never know.

When Nomad and I crossed the border from Georgia to Carolina we stopped for a moment at the sign, and as we did it started to lightly snow, it was beautiful. Together we reached a milestone, a literal one and walked into North Carolina. I watched Nomad reach out one last time to touch the snow-covered sign, he had only seen snow a handful of chances, and this time was with me. We hiked on for eleven miles with snow piling on our shoes, until we set up our tent for the night at Sassafras Gap.

At some hour in the middle of the night our tent collapsed under the weight of the snowstorm. Nomad woke up to find half of the tent buried; luckily it didn't soak into our sleeping bags. In the snow we packed up and hiked 10.2 miles up Standing Indian Mountain, where many other hikers took a fall, and we kept going until after sundown. When it was dark I realized the battery in my headlamp froze from the cold, the short beam of light was barely enough to find a campsite spot along the edges of Beech Gap.

In the morning the weather was still cold and snowy, we made a hasty plan to hike twelve miles towards Rock Gap Shelter to call a shuttle into Franklin North Carolina. The day was rough. We climbed Albert Mountain and a large fire tower, hitting mile marker one hundred on the trail. There were moments I honestly didn't think I was going to make the climb. Albert Mountain was one of the hardest navigating sections, where I was pulling myself up by roots around slippery rocks to reach the summit. All day it was raining or snowing and I kept thinking to myself I might slip too far, but I was lucky I had Nomad looking out for me.

After the incline Nomad and I reached the tower to find the view was completely covered in fog. We climbed the stairs regardless of the scenery and on our descent walked by a tree with a group of rocks underneath placed out by another hiker to form 100.

At Rock Gap Shelter we met two brothers going by the trail names Einstein and Little Cheese, after telling them our plan to head out with a shuttle they packed up their equipment and abandoned their idea of spending a freezing night alone in the shelter. The four of us shared a warm ride and we were dropped off in Franklin North Carolina to find a number of other hikers who all checked in to escape the snow. Nomad and I secured a room at the Budget Inn for the first night and walked over to the Lazy Hiker Brewery to meet up with Pace for her birthday celebration. Outside the brewery we ordered dinner at a food truck, we stood arms outstretched by the heaters waiting for large baskets of quesadillas and fries. Inside I signed the Appalachian Trail Class of 2017 Banner while slowly sipping on apple beers. Everyone gathered around the bar, JW, Wasabi, Pace, Gourmet and Fedora the Explorer.

It was in Franklin North Carolina celebrating the first one hundred miles completed on the trail when I learned how much Nomad and the hike already changed me. We spent all night at the lazy hiker brewery, bought Pace drinks and in the morning ate breakfast in town with JW. We were sitting at the counter looking over the contents to keep in my resupply box, when JW shared, "Raven you surprise me. When we first met at Springer you didn't talk very much or look around, now your always smiling and you meet people in the eye". Nomad nodded and agreed "You can really see her eyes now". Days earlier, in the middle of a snowstorm at Carter Gap Shelter, my glasses broke and became unusable. In Franklin my eyes met others. I was no longer hiding. It was also in Franklin that JW, filling out his trail father role, advised me on Nomad, "It's not just your eyes, I can see into his as well".

When we returned to the mountains the hiker purist in me wanted to head back to the last shelter to retrace the short trail we skipped going into Franklin. I headed alone southbound to where we diverted and bushwhacked to the road days earlier. I walked silently for most of the day and on returning to the north route wasn't able to catch up with Pace, Wasabi or Nomad. With spotty cell service and no hikers in sight I headed as quickly as I could to the nearest shelter. Siler Bald Shelter was marked in the guidebook as a steep .5-mile off trail shelter and the path was awfully difficult to hike down in the ice.

Hiking in the ice, I regretted with every step my decision to hike my own stubborn mile for mile hike alone. I fell a few times on the way to the shelter climbing on the icy decline and was thankful when I saw the familiar faces of hikers Einstein, Little Cheese, who was bundled in his sleeping bag from the cold, and Nomad. I rested my pack for a while on the shelter floor and rested my arms around Nomad. Saying goodbye to Einstein and Little Cheese, Nomad and I decided to hike further and find a camping spot aside the trail. Together we hiked up and out from the icy shelter.

Chapter 5: Food, Water & Shelter

It was icy and cold the day in North Carolina when I lost my glasses. When I woke up in the morning I learned that all my socks were soaked and my shoelaces became frozen chunks of ice. I just barely managed to slam my feet into shoes and wrap my microspikes around the bottom. (I was one of the only hikers I met willing to carry the pound of weight of microspikes. I knew I needed the balance and traction in the snow to counterbalance my ataxia). The weather and conditions were terrible enough that after only hiking three miles reaching Carter Gap Shelter Nomad and I decided to stay.

The weather was below twenty degrees and slowly we watched as the shelter filled after noon until it was packed beyond capacity. In everyone's eagerness to escape the snow inside the shelter we were tightly packed with twelve people in an eight-man shelter. Hikers set up camp sideways and along the floor near a picnic bench under the small overhang. I thought I was roughing it with no dry clothes, I hadn't felt my toes or fingers in days, I carried no stove to cook warm food in, but some hikers wouldn't have a spot in the shelter.

There was talk of climbing underneath the beams of shelter wood in search of space away from the snow. One hiker spent hours at the bench sowing his pants together with floss because he slept on the picnic table, rolled and fell over splitting his pants right down the center. We were just grateful for the light conversation and the escape from the cold within the shelter's walls.

Late in March the snow melted into puddles upon puddles of mud. The puddles were a challenge to avoid (especially for the shorter hikers). Jaybelle, who I met on the approach trail and later again with the hiker bubble, and I compared the amount of mud splattered on the backsides of our legs from falling or sinking deep into the earth. We faced another muddy day on a solid uphill trek to Sassafras Gap Shelter, which became my favorite shelter at two stories holding spots for fourteen hikers.

For hikers a nearby spring was slick, but right next to the shelter for quick and easy access. I found I was always grateful after a long day of hiking in snow, rain or in mud to settle down for the night in a good shelter with friends. At Sassafras Shelter a group of us were joined by a few section hikers and their dog sharing stories and food around the shelters picnic table. Our new friend named Quest passed around drinks and we all watched the sun go down thru the slits in the shelter walls.

I thought Sassafras Gap Shelter was built for the largest trail party, until we hiked to the Fontana Dam. The Fontana "Hilton" Shelter stood impressively alongside the water and was made to fit a total of twenty hikers. Although Nomad and I arrived right after sunset we still admired the solar chargers and sheer size of the campgrounds. By the light of the moon we sat with a large group around the campfire and I was content enough to share the large bag of chips I carried all day on the back of my pack. After everyone's dinner we stored our food bags inside of the anti bear garbage bins. There were at least twenty food bags sitting together at the bottom of the pales, at this shelter no bear bag hanging would be necessary. The best thing about the Hilton was after setting up my sleeping bag I could walk up the hill to use an actual restroom. They had real toilets instead of privies, sinks with running water and even two shower stalls. Our stay at the Hilton was indeed heavenly.

Towards the end of our miles in North Carolina the shelters went from sizable and large like the Hilton, into something else entirely. After summiting Max Patch in the rain, one of the greatest views on the trail standing on top a sweeping bald, I hiked a long day and decided to be ironic and end at Walnut Mountain Shelter. After climbing Walnut Mountain I smiled at the sight of the shelter, which was small, but grand in meaning. Walnut is the name of the first book I ever published, a memoir about my struggle and overcoming the removal of my brain tumor called "Walnut". Although the tumor was removed, I took the life I had and challenged myself. I left behind the girl who was only a dreamer and stopped placing limits on myself.

There I was standing aside Walnut Mountain Shelter in North Carolina after walking over 260 miles on the Appalachian Trail. I looked into the shelter and then down at my guidebook, which placed it as a six-person shelter, there were already five men who seemed skeptic about making room for another, but they did, reluctantly. We spent the night with our feet sticking out enjoying the occasional gust of wind, until the rain and snow came down. In the morning I woke up, realized I lost my rain gear and instead I poked arm and head holes into a black garbage bag. I visited the privy to enjoy the privileges of a roof from the storm and headed down the mountain, thirteen miles into the town of Hot Springs. It was a long day with a steep climb up Bluff Mountain followed by hours of windy switchbacks. The beauty about the day was I only ran into fellow hikers and nobody had a second glance or comment on my garbage bag attire. Maybe there is the meaning behind my hike, I could spend a cold night in a small Walnut Mountain Shelter, walk out in stormy weather wearing a garbage bag and feel nothing but proud.

If I ever have the means I would donate or sponsor the Walnut Shelter as well as the Rich Mountain Lookout Tower. After leaving Hot Springs in North Carolina Nomad and I hiked out of town and we were at Lovers Leap Rock when a large number of day hikers stopped and asked to take a picture with us. For the day we hiked and passed the time eagerly awaiting the view from an upcoming lookout tower. When we finally arrived planning to set up camp and see the view, we were met with closed and boarded off stairs. The tower wasn't the ideal shelter we were looking for, but camping in a nearby field wasn't our worst night stay.

Further on the trail, leaving Erwin in Tennessee Nomad and I hiked a short nine-mile day, stopping for lunch at Curley Maple Gap Shelter. The stream was low and the banks were muddy, I slipped and had to filter my water twice before returning with my trekking pants covered in leaves. The shelter itself was great, but it was too short a distance for our planned miles and with daylight to spare we heard of a nice spot at a field further ahead. We didn't realize until arriving at the field that there was a loud sound coming from an overhead power line. With the forecast calling for rain we looked at our guidebooks, noticing the next shelter was still eight miles away with a climb up Unaka Mountain and into a dense spruce forest. Shaking out heads we set up our tent as far away as we could from the power lines and wished for the best of luck.

We found the occasional bad luck with shelters and provisions throughout our hike and even up north in Maine. While in Millinocket I adopted a large stuffed animal black bear I decided to strap to the back of my pack, hike with and call him Moose. I hoped Moose would bring us good fortune, but we found no mountain berries or legendary bear caves to escape with.

Moose, Nomad and I had high hopes when hearing about trail magic and particularly in an upcoming buffet at Abol Bridge. We planned our miles just in time for breakfast and eagerly left our packs outside the front door. Inside we were met with a near empty display of mini muffins, empty juice pitchers and a tray that may have contained, at one point, scrambled eggs. We sat down to eat what we could and then on our way out were surprised when we were stopped and asked to pay for our fabulous buffet meals. The weight of cash sadly gone from our pockets we readjusted our bug netting and I secured Moose on my pack before entering the hundred-mile wilderness.

Northern hospitality was very different then the southern sections of the Appalachian Trail. In the north even with full on bug netting the black flies immediately surrounded us, it was impossible to stop long enough to filter water. We tried to avoid water but fording streams was inevitable and then the black flies were everywhere. The flies left bites all over my face on the way down from Katahdin and they were marking up the back of my legs in the wilderness. We spent a day trying to hike past the bugs, only briefly stopping at the first baseball bat floor shelter and setting up tent alongside Rainbow Lake. Arriving around sundown we found a new friend Stepping Wolf with his dog Maggie, said hello, went down to the stream for water, cooked dinner and fell immediately asleep. It was difficult for Nomad to cook dinner with all the flies and we would quickly dart back after into the safety of the tent.

Unlike our time in the south, the weather in Maine was humid, rainy and cloudy. At Rainbow Stream Lean-to Nomad and I ate lunch with Stepping Wolf watching for hours while he tried to dry out his gear. It was at Rainbow Stream we realized the shelters were called Lean-to's, tended to have baseball bat flooring (made out of round trees) and had room for generally six people.

Nomad and I hiked in and out of rain, mud, countless black flies and set up tent past an old logging road further up along the trail. We covered miles slowly tripping on the slippery roots and even Nomad fell a few times. We met a ridge runner, climbed two mountains and paused only to look back at Katahdin, under the safety of my umbrella, as the sun was beating down and my hands were starting to burn from lyme disease medication.

Chapter 6: The Smoky Mountains
Never quit on a bad day.

Before the black flies and lyme disease, near the end of our first month on trail my tramily and I walked across the Fontana Dam and into the Smoky Mountains. I enjoyed the stretch at the dam, which was lovely and flat, but then the North Carolina entrance into the Smokies started with an exhausting uphill climb. We hiked slowly that day and not even a mile on the incline Wasabi stopped along the trail, collapsing to her knees. After a break and a phone call to her mother she decided to head back down the mountain. I hugged Wasabi goodbye and the majority of our hiking group headed back down with her. Quest strapped her pack to his front and hiked carrying the weight of two full packs back down to the nearest road crossing along the Fontana Dam.

With my friends headed back and Nomad too far ahead, I was left alone for a few hours on the trail. I thought about how rough the Smoky Mountains were. I thought about Wasabi quitting, possibly leaving the hike forever, and I doubted the trail until I came upon the Shuckstack Fire Tower. After the incline, a small wood and metal building stood before me with a surrounding view out at the mountains. At the base I dropped my pack and smiled at the sight of my favorite thing, I adore fire towers. I skipped around to avoid the bees, held onto the one secure railing and climbed up the winding stairs. 78 steps I took up the tower and I felt the building sway beneath me with every other step.

I was surprised, I was warned by southbound hikers to avoid the aging tower, but I felt invigorated by the climb.

At the towers summit I stopped to look out at the Smoky Mountains, I admired the difficult trail I had taken following south back to the Fontana Dam and I could see heading north where I was going next. At that moment alone on the top of the tower I let go of all my doubts. I decided to do something spontaneous and silly, I howled as loudly as I could out to the mountains. I announced I was there and I heard the echo in my heart call back to say *I'm doing this beautiful crazy thing.*

At the end of my first day hiking in the Smoky Mountains, miles after the fire tower, I caught up with Nomad chatting with a young man named Shades and we camped out near Ekaneetlee Gap. The following day we hiked on to and stayed at our first shelter in the Smokies called Rusell Field Shelter. At the shelter Nomad and I were reunited again with Teach, who hiked heavy miles to catch back up on the trail. The Smokies, we learned from Teach, are very different from what we knew about the trail.

In the Smokies the shelters are large, made of stone with fireplaces and space enough to sleep fourteen hikers. In the mountains, short distance and weekenders have priority spots and thru hikers are required to set up tents when possible. The Shelters themselves were spacious, but very dusty (we fell sick for days after) and the worst news was the complete absence of privies. Instead of privies, The Smokies have designated fields that are intended for use as the bathroom.

Since the beginning and the day Wasabi left, every moment in the Smoky Mountains seemed harder then the last. After Russel Field, we made low miles stopping for the next night at Derrick Knob Shelter. The inclines and elevation changes were hard to keep up with. I fell three times during the day on a combination of descents into mud and rocks. At one point I fell on my knees and was unaware that my elbow was injured as well until I went to take another step, but couldn't bend my arm to extend my trekking pole. Towards the end of the day we found our friend Jaybelle, who was also hiking slow, carrying enough food given to her from section hikers to bypass the next trail town of Gatlinburg complexly. Nomad and I were planning on stopping in town and while we were running low on food we counted down the hours in dusty packed shelters nibbling on our poptarts until we could hitch a ride into town.

Before mile marker 200 we decided to leave the trail for the parking lot at Clingman's Dome (the highest point on the A.T). By the time we reached the lot the sun was going down, Nomad and I didn't realize until we called for a shuttle that the access road was closed until April and that was days away. No vehicles were allowed past the locked gate and nobody could possibly reach us for a ride. Anxious and determined, Nomad and I walked seven miles after sundown, down the deserted road past the gate where luckily a taxi agreed to park.

At the roads end an amazing woman had received our call for help and even though we had no idea the hours it would take, she waited with the engine warm and waiting for us. Our shuttle driver graciously drove us into the town of Gatlinburg where we were taken aback by the scene. After a stark comparison from hiking in the woods the town at night looked, to me, like a miniature Las Vegas. The restaurants and attractions amid the streets were booming with flashing lights illuminating the vast number of tourists walking on the sidewalks without packs or hiking gear. We felt out of place at once, but were glad for a place to rest our packs, a warm hotel room and two extra large cheesy boxes of pizza. In the morning I heard from Teach and we moved our gear to the other side of Gatlinburg, to Motel Six for a zero day in town.

From Teach we learned that Pace and Quest were back behind us hiking the trail in the Smokies. We missed hiking with the rest our friends, but worse then that we missed saying one last goodbye to Wasabi. In Gatlinburg she finalized her decision to quit the hike, her family arrived in town and she left the trail behind her.

After contemplating laundry and resupply food shopping, Nomad and I had dinner with Teach, drinks and double chocolate cheesecake at a restaurant in town. Before the trail, even as a New Yorker, I did not sincerely enjoy cheesecake, but the trail provides and the cake was divine. Hiker hunger is real, Nomad ate four orders of macaroni and cheese and along with the cake we listened to a local band preform for hours before returning to our motel.

In the morning the three of us hitched a ride back to the trail using Teaches "Hiker to Trail" sign. It was harder then usual to hitch a ride with a vehicle large enough for three hikers and our packs while we were so far from the trail. Several tourists passing through Gatlinburg didn't even know it's a possible spot for backpackers to stop at. We were lucky though, a trail angel in a jammed car made space enough for the three of our packs and us to journey back to the mountains.

At the parking lot to the trail standing underneath the sign, which divides North Carolina and the Tennessee state line, we said our goodbyes. Teach headed on north and we headed back south to Clingman's Dome, I was still holding a purist mind set and we agreed the highest point of the Appalachian Trail was a milestone that no hiker should miss. At sundown Nomad and I reached the spot, right before a rainstorm, we stood together under the dome with the wind whipping around us. We were the last ones to hike Clingman's for the day and since we knew the parking lot and road were closed, we knew just how to avoid the rainstorm.

Nomad and I spent the night stealth camping on the freshly cleaned parking lot restroom floor. Our two sleeping pads and bags fit perfectly along the walls and it easily became one of our best stealth camping spots on the trail (later on was Baxter State Park). We had a roof over our heads and one of the best nights of sleep we could hope for, until we heard the park rangers roll up in the morning. With the sun peaking in through the windows we quietly packed our bags, put on our rain gear and slipped out back into the woods.

Unfortunately, backtracking and doubling up on miles to retrace our steps to and from Clingmans Dome became tiring. When we reached the next parking lot Nomad decided he wanted to hitch to find a ride to spend another night back in Gatlinburg. In the end I went back with him and we stayed with our friends BB and Magic Mic at a motel on another side of town. In the familiar pattern of ours we did laundry and consumed several meals in town until the following day. In the morning we were lucky to find another hitch with a photographer heading out to take trail pictures and he dropped us back again at the state line and New Found Gap. Viewing the trail map Nomad and I decided to take a short day of hiking with low miles, stopping for lunch at Icewater Shelter and camping at night near Porters Gap.

Feeling exhausted in the morning, from all the trips to town and back to the trail, I hiked slowly the next day by myself stopping at intervals to catch my breath and adjust the weight in my pack. The Smoky Mountains were wearing on me, step by slowly planned step, hours later I reached The Tri Corner Knob Shelter and found Nomad's entry in the logbook. Nomad stopped at the shelter before lunch and wrote that he was hoping to reach the next shelter miles ahead on the trail by nightfall. Unlike my friend, I had no strong ambition that my legs could carry me even one mile further on the mountains. I set up my gear in the corner of the shelter, ate dinner with the other hikers and fell restlessly asleep.

In the morning everyone gathered around the picnic table worrying about a storm that was heading in. A family of weekenders with their children bundled up, putting on gloves and arguing over the cold. Zipping up my jacket I settled on a quick breakfast gave an encouraging smile to the young kids and headed out early with no plan in mind. With no set goal, I ended up hiking my longest day in the Smokies of over eighteen miles. Back early in the morning I passed my first shelter before the storm really hit down, with rain and snow the trail became a sleeted river. Under the cover of a tree I attached my trekking umbrella to a strap below my collarbone and hiked on up another steady incline. I was miles away from any shelter when I was hit with a large whipping gust of wind. The wind was strong, my hands tried to hold shaking to my trekking poles for balance and I forgot to grab hold of the umbrella.

In an instant the wind shook my umbrella, breaking the adjustment piece attaching it to my pack and causing half to fold in and tear away off sight of the trail. With no dry clothing left I had no choice but to keep moving north, getting soaked in the rain. At one point I looked down at the map and realized I could either stop at a shelter soaked for the night, or if I kept going I could reach the Standing Bear Hostel just outside the Smokies. I stomped thru knee high streams and miles upon miles for a warm bed to crawl into and a solid roof overhead. The day I left the Smokies, at a rock overlook I climbed to the top and took one last look at the mist covered ridges and I was gone. The moment I stepped out from the Smoky Mountains at Davenport Gap the rain stopped, the clouds parted and I took a picture of the first flowers I had seen in days. I took off my jacket and looked up at the sun, it was a cliché moment out of a picture book, I said goodbye to the Smoky Mountains.

I followed the gravel road up hill and with luck I caught the very last bunk left at Standing Bear Hostel. A large group of hikers gathered around the campfire as I visited the store and purchased my dinner of tortillas and a Twix bar. I couldn't remember the last time I held a Twix bar, suddenly I found myself lost in it, the most amazing crafted food in the world. After my dinner and right before sundown Nomad, having found the remnants of my trekking umbrella on the trail, arrived at Standing Bear.

Chapter 7: Hostels

Standing Bear was a classic hostel atmosphere, I found myself in a bunkroom filled with hikers listening to the fire crackling outside along with the twang of a nearby guitar. Right around the border between Tennessee and North Carolina the boys outside were toasting beers and singing country songs about thumbing their way to North Caroline.

In Robbinsville North Carolina Nomad and I were hiking along the Appalachian Trail when we found a card leaning on a ledge for a nearby hostel. Stecoah Gap Wolf Creek Hostel was offering to pick up hikers and shuttle them into town for a night stay at a decent hiker rate price. Their offer was further temping to both of us when we heard about an incoming thunderstorm, looked up at the next steep incline called Jacobs Ladder and decided our hike could resume in the morning. We sat on a picnic bench beside the road watching the clouds roll in and made the call. The owner of the hostel, a very nice man with trail magic fruit in the trunk of his car brought us down the road to his place at Wolf Creek Hostel.

The first two to arrive for the night, we had our pick of rooms, shower and laundry room. We walked down the hill from the hostel to a small country store where we found pasta and biscuits to cook for dinner. Back at the hostel we cooked on a real four-burner stove, used the oven and shared our extra biscuits with a young girl and her father who were hiking the trail. The young girl injured her foot on the mountain and the two were packing in to leave the trail for an unknown time. We chatted for hours, hoping an early recovery for her, until the storm hit down strong, the hostel lost power and we fell asleep to the sounds of thunder, safe in our warm roof covered home for the duration of a night.

In the morning we walked back down to the country store and sat on benches for an amazing breakfast, the best pancakes I have ever eaten. After a perfect meal we packed our bags, The Mayor, the hostel owners donned trail name, dropped us off at the trail. Because we were well rested and fed, conquering Jacobs Ladder was a walk in the park for Nomad and I. We passed another hiker who was breathing hard, stopping frequently on the way up and he could barely introduce himself. When we took a break later in the day for a lunch of fresh fruit from the hostel we couldn't keep from smiling. Struggling tales of Jacob's Ladder were shared for months and we would laugh, for us, our night at Wolf Creek Hostel made all the difference.

When we reached Erwin Tennessee I had sunburn all down my legs and fell into bad luck breaking the straps on my trail shoes walking into town. (The hiker solution for anything broken is in the reliability of duct tape and my sunburn legs would just suffer). After contemplating laundry Nomad and I ordered pizza and fell immediately asleep in the warm hotel room. In the morning we walked around town and I decided to have my hair cut off and donated at a local hair salon. The weather was turning too warm for long hair; it was impossible to manage without the ability to shower everyday. With my new pixie hair we met up with Pace, Quest and Teach at a Mexican Restaurant before staying at Uncle Johnnies Hostel for the night. Uncle Johnnies was packed with familiar faces and we were lucky enough to secure our own private room and a shuttle back from the restaurant at night.

When I walked into Hampton Tennessee I looked around for restaurants and then headed over to the local grocer who recommended I cross the street and check into the Braemar Castle Hostel. For the small amount of cash left in my pocked I booked a bed in the bunkroom and dinner, which became pasta alfredo, the largest bag I could find of barbeque chips and ice-cream. I fell asleep that night, after washing my clothes in the sink, to the unfortunate sound of an entire neighborhood of barking dogs, drifting in from the open hostel window.

In the spring rain was as common as was our search for hostels to avoid the rain in. When Nomad and I reached Pearisburg Virginia we set our goal on Woods Hole Hostel. I reserved us a private room for the night by calling ahead just when we hit a lucky spot of cell phone reception on the trail. We arrived right before sundown and were greeted affectionately by the owner who welcomed us, "Are you Raven and Nomad? Come around back we are just about to serve dinner." Neville, one of the hostel owners, was cooking an exceptional meal with a large pot of soup, macaroni and cheese, homemade bread and ice-cream for all the hikers. We sat on the front porch enjoying the food with over twenty hikers gathering around tables. After our homemade ice cream desert Nomad and I went to sleep in a private high ceiling room upstairs.

In the morning we read a forecast of further rain, found warm comfortable robes on our closet doors and decided to take a zero day at Woods Hole. In the robes we walked down to the main room for a hostel specialty home cooked breakfast. At the bottom of the stairs the glasses of orange juice were all in line to spell out AT for the trail. The group of hikers from the bunkhouse and private rooms met with the owners to enjoy a meal of cooked eggs and fruit cobbler. Before we ate we stood in a circle holding hands with one another while Neville suggested thinking of what we were thankful for. Nomad and I agreed we were both thankful for zero days and warm robes.

As the hikers piled out for their day hiking in the rainy woods, we spent the hours inside away from the storm playing with the hostels cats and watching episodes of tiny house hunters while Nomad fixed a computer. For lunch I had a pint of Neville's homemade cookie dough ice cream and for dinner, pasta with homemade bread and additional ice cream. The following morning, in return for Nomad's computer expertise, the hostel helped us out with private shuttle arrangements and a pack to use for our first experience into slackpacking.

No Pain No Rain No Maine. In Maine, Nomad and I shared a shelter on a rainy night with four new southbounders who mentioned plans to stop at a hostel within the one hundred mile wilderness called White

House Landing. Originally we didn't know there was a hostel within the wilderness, we planned a food drop and miles to pass on without stopping.

On our way down the mountain we were caught in the middle of a hail thunderstorm and were soaked before we could put our packs down to get out our rain Packas. We were only just starting to dry off with the miles when the guidebook called for forging two strong streams. Grudgingly we took off our hiking shoes and muddy socks to slowly make our way through the water to the other side. I tried to keep my balance, but couldn't walk across the rapid waters, I sat down between fallen tree logs and wrapped my knees around them inching slowly to the other side. While forging the stream, listening to the sounds of the current pushing in, I began to feel lightheaded trying to make progress to the other side. I stopped several times trying to hear Nomad's voice over the water, swatting the bugs away, noticing the streaks of blood down my arms, neck and chest. My slow progress attracted hoards of Maine's eager black flies and I had twenty or more on each of my arms. Distracted and dizzy I swayed on a branch and almost fell while reaching for Nomad's arm on the other side of the swift stream.

After a surprise hailstorm, forging two streams and living with Maine's black flies we reached a sign and the dock for White House Landing. At the dock I called for the boat and four of us hikers hitched a ride over to the hostel. At the old campground we stayed in a cabin with no electric or water, we did our laundry from a pump and had dinner at the main house where everything ran off propane. At the counter we ordered pizza and sat around with a couple on their honeymoon along with other hikers.

In the morning staring out at the one hundred mile wilderness and incoming rainstorm from our cabin, we decided to take a zero day. We cooked rice and I read a book for hours sitting along the front porch. In the morning we saw our first moose and decided it was time to leave Maine behind.

Chapter 8: Zero Days

On reaching Hot Springs in North Carolina I reserved two nights at the Laughing Hart Hostel right aside the Appalachian Trail. I went thru my normal hiker town routine, visited the post office for a mail drop, resupply meals at the grocery store and finished an entire cheese pizza at the local diner. I was walking along the outfitters and various shops when Quest from an upstairs building called out to me. I went up to visit and check out Quest, Teaches and Nomad's place as well as to borrow a book, A Midnight Summers Dream, from the library.

During my zero day in Hot Springs my brother, his two dogs, his coworker and her dog stopped in for a visit. I was lucky he was traveling from Texas back to New York and he thought it would be nice to detour to visit with me. I hadn't seen my brother since the winter holiday and he didn't recognize me at first dressed in my hiking gear. While in town I showed him around the hostel and the six of us (dogs included) had lunch out on the patio of a local restaurant. Cyrus, my brothers, dog took to barking at every hiker he met carrying trekking poles. After the meal, we walked a few miles on the trail north and then back again to the parking lot. We followed the trail markers, which were along the sidewalks of town. I held onto Cassandra's leash while we paused to take a picture at a white blaze aside the water. Before my brother went to leave we stopped for amazing ice cream, orange chocolate chip, at an art café near the edge of town.

Back at the hostel minus my brother, I ran into Quest, Teach and Nomad who were checking into the building. Together we huddled around on a bench outside in the cold until we decided to head down to the tavern for drinks. Unfortunately by the evening I was in the middle of doing laundry and waiting for my hiking clothes to finish air-drying. Not wanting to miss out on the opportunity, I went out into town wearing borrowed clothes, fluffy pink pajama bottoms and a large black hoodie. I was cold, but it was a hiker town and nobody said a thing.

Back during my first zero day in Franklin I had breakfast with Nomad and JW at the Kountry Kitchen. We sat at the counter and I ordered my usual sweet tea with biscuits and gravy (sometimes without the gravy if it wasn't vegetarian). In between biscuit eating I opened a mail drop from my mother and we enjoyed the smiley faces and words of encouragement written all along the sides. Nomad and I then moved our packs to the other side of town to share a hotel room at the Comfort Inn with Pace, Wasabi and Quest. We had a nice shuttle driver who never asked for money and ate with us at a nearby Chinese buffet. After the buffet we walked over to the store for resupply and ended up for a second night at the Lazy Hiker Brewery for trivia night. I ordered one drink before I realized I was tired of the bar, the drinking and I missed the miles along the trail. Instead of calling for our shuttle I walked the 2.7 miles back to the hotel, it was consolation that even on a zero day I could still put in town miles.

My second zero day in Franklin was unwanted, I

finished my resupply the day before, enjoyed a shower, consumed enough cooked food and wanted to head back to the trail. I stayed in town another day because it was cold, snowy and my hiking companions were hungover. In the middle of the night I woke up to use the bathroom and ended up cleaning piles of hair covering the entire floor, when they came back from the brewery shaving a few heads of hair was on their agenda. I found comfort cleaning up the bathroom, fell back into the bed and decided to hangout the following day with Jaybelle and JW.

In the morning we went to the outfitters where I purchased a new pair of winter gloves and a souvenir shirt, which I shipped back home. Then the three of us found a coffee shop bar where I sat with a warm apple cider while thinking about my longing to be back on the trail. After the cider, JW and I headed to Mulligans for lunch and fried pickles, walked around the town and then went out again in the late evening for a few pizzas.

After our night in the Fontana "Hilton" Shelter we caught a shuttle into town and had breakfast at the Fontana Village Resort. My tramily booked a small house with a private hot tub in the town of Robbinsville and we brooded in the lobby for a while wondering how to get a ride there. Robbinsville is not a typically listed trail town and we were not a typical small group looking for a ride. Seeing six of us waiting a kind woman, whose nephew was hiking the trail, offered us rides and drove two trips to get all our packs and us into town.

While waiting for our friends Nomad, Pace and I enjoyed lunch at Lynn's Restaurant in the middle of Robbinsville, I had no idea portabella mushroom fries existed and I was grateful to discover they were amazing. Once the second shuttle dropped off our remaining tramily we were in search of a new ride to our rented house. After stopping for groceries, we met a man who shared he was an original Appalachian Trail hiker by the name of Quest. Quest was also the name of one of the men in our tramily and we were thankful for the ride in the back of his pick up truck. When we were dropped off, after looking around the place, I found a nice grassy field by the water and lay there while the others took showers and contemplated the hot tub. Pace put together a salad and there was enough pizza and drinks for the night.

In the morning feeling the opposite of how one should feel after a zero day at a private hot tub bed and breakfast, Nomad and I decided to spend a second zero day closer into town at the San Ran Motel. After checking in we walked around, went to a few thrift stores where I found a temporary town jacket for the cold and we had lunch at the nearby café. Exploring around the town a stray dog followed us for some time, then we reorganized our packs and went out again to dinner outside at a place called The Hub. We played chess, (I lost) shared nicely cooked macaroni and cheese followed by a desert of warm heated brownies drizzled in chocolate sauce.

Chapter 9: The Virginia Blues

I lost a chance for warm cooked food when I
missed out on trail magic, I watched the car drive away
before me as the rain rolled in. I hiked too slowly one
morning heading out from a shelter, everyone else
would talk about the trail magic and I missed it. After
feeling sorry for my luck I called my brother from my
cell phone to wish him a happy birthday and then I ran
into a friend of Teaches who was hiking southbound to
meet up with him. It was ironic because the hiker
stopped to chat and was telling me about the trail magic
and his friend with a corn allergy until I started
laughing, "Do you mean Teach?" Before heading our
separate ways I reminded him to meet later on with
Teach and the rest of our tramily at Trail Days in
Virginia.

I spent the rest of my morning walking potato less
(still mourning the loss of trail magic) thru a gorgeous
farm field in the rain. In-between raindrops I climbed
fence stys and had lunch with a few hikers in a packed
shelter while they too hoped to wait out the rain. The
group of boys was sprawled out on the shelter floor
discussing hiking long miles into the nearby town of
Damascus Virginia. Before the rain ended two slack
packers jovially skipped by on the trail singing
"Damascus Damascus were going into town for pizza".
I was reminded of my long mile hike out of The
Smokies and suddenly I found myself putting in longer
miles, passing the shelters and campsites, the TN-VA
border and there I was walking under the notorious

sign "Welcome to Damascus".

I arrived in the town at sundown and unsure of where to go I walked along the trail around the village and stopped when I heard guitar music strumming peacefully outside. I found myself at The Broken Fiddle Hostel; with one room left I settled in for the night and fell asleep.

The following day Nomad caught up into Damascus and we met for lunch at Alfredo's Restaurant. The meal was so delicious that we bought the chef milk to cook extra sauce with when the restaurant was out of it weeks later during Trail Days. After the first Alfredo meal, at the outfitters I decided it was time to retire my beat up hiking shoes, I purchased new non water proof trail runners and discarded my old shoes in the hostel's hiker box. The Hostel was the most festive place in entire town; there wasn't a moment a group of hikers weren't gathered around outside laughing enjoyably or playing music. A group of us hikers watched movies in the living room while a few made large quantities of chili to last all night long.

Leaving Damascus Nomad and I walked a short while along the Virginia Creeper Trail before the trail met up with the Appalachian Trail. On the Creeper Trail we were passed in the rain by several bikers whizzing briefly by us. The Virginia Creeper felt serene with bridges overlooking the trail and water. In the rain the bikers looked anything but happy, they seemed miserable to be caught out in the rain, in such a beautiful place. We were sad when it was time to turn back into the woods and we stopped for the day at

Saunders Shelter. There were rumors about Saunders Shelter and recent bear sightings, we met a few tenters, but Nomad and I were the only hikers to stay that night inside the shelter (apart from the mice, who seemed unruffled by the bear sightings).

With the weather forecast of solid rain for a week our plans changed into traveling short distances at low mileage and staying within shelters or shelter hopping as the hikers call it. The holiday (4/20) seemed to make a lot of the hikers slow down and as we were walking we stopped to notice the date spelled out by a hiker before us in rocks along the trail. With the bad timing of pace, rain and mud we hiked to Thomas Knob shelter where we were met with weathered and mud soaked wild ponies. The wild ponies are known to roam the Grayson Highlands and although Nomad and I tried to be prepared, we forgot to bring food for them. The ponies were hanging out at the shelter all day licking the rocks and attempting to befriend hikers who remembered to bring them apples.

Nomad and I set up our sleeping bags in the shelter upstairs to keep our gear out of sight from getting eaten by the ponies and then we slackpacked to Mt. Rogers, Virginia's highest peak at 5,729 ft. The hike wasn't difficult, but the summit was somewhat disappointing, we stood in the middle of a forest and looked down at the elevation marker wishing that there had been a fire tower or at least a view. Back at the shelter we watched a movie upstairs on our phones until a few hikers settled in below us, heard noises and assumed we were ghosts in the attic. Upon realizing there was a ladder and people on the second floor we were joined for the night by Einstein and his brother Little Cheese.

In the middle of the night, I was laying on my side facing the wall when I heard, inches from my face, a group of mice growl at me. Nomad awoke in the dark to find me clutching in fear to his sleeping bag, shaking. I did not sleep for the rest of the night.

The next day we were hoping to meet several other wild ponies within the Grayson Highlands, but saw nothing until we passed mile marker 500, which a hiker displayed out on the trail using balls of pony poop. (How or with what they picked up and strategically placed the poop one can only imagine). After the marker, the rain started coming down and when we reached Wise Shelter it was completely packed with hikers escaping the rain. There was no room to sit or dry out equipment and fifteen hikers from a college freshmen wilderness class tried to miserably pile in with everyone else.

Back on the trail, unable to remain in the shelter for long, Nomad and I both took turns slipping on the rain soaked trail. After falling and sliding into a large pile of mud, completely soaking my legs, we were ecstatic to find trail magic at The Scales Livestock Corral. A group of fishermen set up large canopies around a fire with camp chairs, cooked food and the most amazing southern hospitality. They invited a group of us hikers to sit down for as long as we like, I had plates of nachos dipped in hot boiling cheese and freshly baked pecan pie.

In Marion Nomad and I spent several zero days and nights recovering from sickness and the rain. At the time we thought it was from stopping in town for Japanese food, but we ended up hearing several complaints from hikers who fell ill after staying at Thomas Knob Shelter. Perhaps it was the rain, the mud, the weather, the ponies or the water source; perhaps it was from a combination of conditions, we were all sick. We spent our first night at the edge of town at a Comfort Inn, where we had a free breakfast in the morning of waffles and apples. We went shopping for resupply at Walmart before walking to our next night stay at the Royal Inn. Walking with our packs soaking in the rain, a kind woman pulled over in a mini van and offered us a ride to the motel. We checked in for the low price of forty bucks to the only availability, a smoking room and had a highlight of food ordered from a restaurant called Macado's.

Back at the motel we attempted to dry our clothes and do bathtub laundry in the small corner bathroom. Unfortunately the room was cold and not one of the clothes dried by the following day. With little sleep, feeling ill and in wet clothes, going back to the trail seemed impossible.

Nomad and I walked back into town and found ourselves at the elegant General Francis Marion Hotel. The stark opposite of the Royal Inn, we spent the next two nights basking in it's glory until we felt well enough to return to the trail. I had the most amazing Caprese Panini, fruit and peanut butter pie at the café across the street from our new hotel. We ordered pizza from 27

Lions and met Mr. Pickles while eating macaroni and cheese at The Wooden Pickle Restaurant. Mr. Pickles, we learned, is a mascot cat that roams around the town of Marion, he has a tendency to hide under the restaurant sign and jump out to hiss at not only hikers, but everyone passing by in his town.

When it was time for us to leave Marion we started walking to the Walmart shuttle, when we were picked up by a caring man in a truck who stopped for us and another hiker offering a ride to the Mt. Rogers visitor center. We hiked seven miles for the day, climbing Glade Mountain and crossing a stream, which was impossible without getting wet shoes, and met friends at Chatfield Shelter. Small enough for six hikers with a picnic table in front aside a great view of the stream, Nomad and I decided to stay for the night. The entertainment was in watching each passing hiker decide how they would tackle crossing the stream. A few took their hiking shoes off completely, one switched out for camp shoes and the rest strode through, as if it was nothing.

While watching the show Nomad and I shared dinner meals around the table with Tin Cup, Hot Tea and Fedora The Explorer. A few others joined us in the shelter and we agreed to meet again the next morning for trail magic at the schoolhouse. In the morning we hiked over gorgeous Virginian fields and met up at the Lindamood School House where a sign for hiker trail magic was nailed to a nearby tree and packs lined the porch of the small once used schoolhouse. Walking in we were greeted by our friends drinking cans of soda and perusing the buckets filled with trail magic. They had everything hiker essential, band-aids, hand sanitizer, toothbrushes, carabineers, you name it.

We sat for a while at the old school desks and read the chalkboard at the front of the room where the date went back to October 7th in the 1800's. Written on the middle board under a framed picture of George Washington were the classes: Math (Arithmetic), Reading (English), Spelling, Science, History, Geography and Music. The chalkboard on the far right next to a strategically placed American Flag contained a scrawled written message.

"Welcome to the 1894 Lindamood one room school, built in 1874. One teacher taught grades 1-9. School started in October and ended March. Usually there were 19-25 students. Teachers were paid 30.00 a month. This school closed in 1937. Have a great day and God bless!"

After signing the trail logbook our hiking group hastily avoided the porch bees, used the old outhouses, one labeled for boys, the other for girls, and we hiked on. In the afternoon we reached Atkins Virginia and stopped for lunch at the Red Barn Restaurant not far from the trail. As a last minute idea after eating the five of us hitched a ride further into town and booked a room at the Comfort Inn. There was no laundry at the hotel, but we did have a shower, comfortable beds and dinner at The Tank Restaurant.

Leaving Atkins we hiked past an interesting spot called the Davis Path campsite and found a completely random privy on the trail. Nomad and I set up tents for the night right before the quarter way mark on the trail along a nearby stream and ate dinner together on a large fallen tree. The trail in Virginia inspired us we hiked along field after field, took pictures at the quarter way mark and stopped in at The Quarter Way Inn. At the inn we met the owner and her dog, spent some time on resupply and enjoyed the view overlooking the vast green farms.

In Bland Virginia Nomad and I stopped at Subways for lunch, picked up additional trail resupply at Trent's Grocery and ordered a pizza to go. We checked in for the night at a hostel where we signed the kitchen wall in marker along side other hikers. The owner had resupply packages for both of us from our families, we were laden down with food and immediately shared around a package of chocolate with a fellow hiker named Slumberland. Post Easter packages are the best; I lived off chocolate and Easter Grass Licorice for days.

We headed back to the trail in the morning with Slumberland, Nomad and I sitting in the back of the hostel owner's truck. We started the day adding on .6 side trail miles to visit Dismal Falls, it was well worth the uncounted mileage with gorgeous views, the perfect spot to stop and have an apple. After visiting Wapiti Shelter there was a steep climb followed by rocky trail until we reached our destination for the night.

One morning after the rocky trails, feeling weighed down, Nomad and I decided to try Virginian Slackpacking. We found a way to shuttle our packs ahead on the trail and then hike with a daypack to a place called the Captains. Nomad and I shared a bright pink slackpack filled with food, water, a water filter and the empty space absence of sunscreen. Feeling lighter we took our time and explored around Pearisburg and an adjacent trail graveyard. On leaving the graveyard we met a man on the trail who asked if he could interview us as hikers. After the interview we stopped to filter water and continue on north. We passed our first shelter when the hikers going south started to comment, "Hey girl…I think your burning". Sure enough the pink pack wasn't as high on my shoulders as my usual backpack and my back was severely burned for months.

The Captains, our destination for the night, was the yard of a very generous man known to the hiker community as The Captain. He allows backpackers to camp in his yard, use his outdoor electric outlets to charge phones, provides picnic tables, water and sodas stocked on his own porch fridge. To reach The Captains hikers place their pack on a hook and take a zip line over a stream, we cooked our dinner on the benches petting The Captain's dog and watching hikers come over on the zip line. After a shared dinner of pasta primavera and mini m&m's Nomad and I set up our tent along a row of other hikers matching tents. I couldn't sleep though; the sunburn on my back was too severe to move. In the morning I welcomed the cold that arrived with the first cloudy sunlight. Every hiker looked chilled with their leggings on underneath shorts and anticipating the cold rain called for later on in the day.

While the burns on my back settled Nomad and I climbed to enjoy the infamous views from McAffe's Knob. Nomad wanted to dangle from the edge, but the disapproval of four thru hikers shot him down. Instead we ate lunch over the side, saw a deer near the trail and headed down to celebrate at a nearby Cracker Barrel Restaurant. After our first dinner we went out with another hiker named Tater for Cinco de Mayo. We sat down in the back of the restaurant listening to music, drinking mango margaritas and eating quesadillas.

Nomad and I took a few zero days in Daleville while my back sunburn bubbled and then started to flake away. At the local town thrift store I went looking for a sweatshirt to hide my burned back while in town and found irony in wearing a NY New York hoodie bought in Virginia. I even started to think of the Howard Johnson we were staying at as our home, we did laundry, rented a car, went to the movies to see Beauty and the Beast and drove to Charlotte NC for an event. I experienced my first and hopefully last meal at Taco Bell, amazing soup at Outback Steakhouse, The Chinese Buffet and Pizza Hut on one of our last nights wearing my NY tourist attire.

Back on the trail we hiked through more of Virginia's gorgeous fields and planted carrots under a gnome farm tree. We spent a night in the nearby shelter with two hikers named Bear Slayer and Yogi. Together we compared the condition of the bottoms of our feet and attempted to roast honey buns over the campfire. At Wilson Creek we met a hiker who was taking his second zero day at the shelter, he was huddled in his sleeping bag recovering from the flu. After hiking in and out of the rain and spending time at the shelter, I felt my pace slowing down and the flu catching on.

In Buchanan Nomad and I had lunch with a hiker who offered to give us a hitch to a motel on the outskirts of town. I had trouble breathing for a day and spent the downtime sleeping at the hotel and discovering that certain Caesar dressing does indeed have anchovies in it.

In Buena Vista we rented another car to explore the nearby historical towns of Lexington and Natural Bridge. We found another Macado's Restaurant in Lexington (reminiscent of our time in Marion) and walked around town to the famous graveyard. In Natural Bridge we visited the Pink Cadillac Diner with the car mascot out in front and I learned that Dr. Pepper is not at all similar to Root Beer. At night we went to the drive in movie theater for double features to see the movies Chips and The Guardians of the Galaxy 2.

On trail after town, we ran into Bear Slayer hiking with Yogi and set up our tent for the night on top Bald Knob, which was a tough climb, but not actually a bald. At the road crossing a car driving by stopped and a man asked if we heard of a hiker named Raven. He was looking for me and was actually following my hike progress online. We shook hands (not the traditional hiker fist bump) and he pointed out the thicket of poison oak I had my pack sitting on.

After hiking .6 miles off the A.T for water at a spring we faced another long day to reach Seeley

Woodworth Shelter. Still feeling under the weather I was having a hard time hiking at a steady pace, keeping up with the miles and dealing with any sort of incline. At Seeley the shelter was packed and in the rain, two dogs unfortunately came inside and joined us.

At the Priest Shelter it is hiker tradition to write confessions within the shelter log book. Usually at the shelter Nomad and I signed our names, commented on the weather and left music lyrics or passing thoughts. Here we spent the day reading our fellow hikers confessions to not practicing leave no trace, yellow blazing, brown blazing, wanting to quit, stealth camping, dramatic trail stalking and the occasional dangerous hitch into town. We wrote our own confessions underneath the last and signed our names, which was a rarity to find hikers willing to own up to their admissions. I started mine "Dear Appalachian Trail Gods forgive me for I have sinned…"

Along the Blue Ridge Parkway we drank Dr. Pepper, met a nice lady who brought us to a small gas station/convenience store for fresh cheese and we spent time at The Royal Oaks Cabins. Later in town at the Chinese Buffet in Waynesboro we met two brothers hiking together from New York. We joked about how the hikers in the restaurant, five of us, were placed in a separate seating area at the buffet. Did we smell? We must have, we were seated at the opposite end of anyone that might be considered a normal restaurant patron. At the motel after our meal we ran into Lempsip and Rictic and made plans to hopefully catch up with them after the Shenandoah's in Harpers

Ferry West Virginia.

Nomad and I rented a car in town, made plans to meet up with our tramily and drove back down state for Trail Days in Damascus Virginia. Near the Grayson Highlands we swung by to pick up Pace and set up for two nights at Rivers Edge Lodging. We reunited the tramily with Quest, Fedora and Gourmet at our place, which was right along Main Street. We made a barbecue and played cards all night with Teach and everyone that stopped by.

At the thrift store in town I found my new hiking shirt, two dollars, green and underarmour displaying a Virginia local sports team on the front. Along the field in town vendors, tents, music and countless hikers gathered for the weekend. In a raffle I won a brand new pair of La Sportiva hiking shoes, bought numerous trail stickers for my nalgene bottles and tried the best southern mixed berry lemonade. I found Cedar Tree, who I hadn't seen since Georgia, and wore my new fitting Packa rain gear in the hiker parade during a spontaneous rainstorm. Our tramily joined the parade with the other hikers from the year 2017 and marched through the streets of Damascus while spectators tossed water balloons and sprayed us with hoses as we passed by. We were nearing the end of the route on the street when it started to down pour and every hiker cheered and whooped, hollering up at the rain.

At the end of Trail Days Nomad, Gourmet and I left Damascus, picked up a thru hiker hitching his way to Marion and headed back north. We all had lunch at Macado's, shared stories, and dropped off one hiker and then Gourmet in Daleville. Back in Waynesboro where we left off on the trail, Nomad and I returned the rent a car and entered the Shenandoah National Park. We had an interesting night at Calf Mountain Shelter where, staying in from the rain, we found the shelter to ourselves.

Once settled in we shared potato chips and stories with the tenting weekenders, before falling asleep upstairs in the shelter. In the morning we passed by Einstein and Little Cheese who were slackpacking southbound to spend the night back at a hostel in Waynesboro. It was a rainy, cloudy day making the views seem non-existent along the trail.

At Blackrock Hut Nomad and I packed in and spent another rainy night listening to the melody of a harmonica player along with the sounds of thunder. At six in the morning we woke up abruptly and headed out for the day, after miles in the rain we reached the Loft Mountain Wayside where we stopped for food. The Wayside seemed to be designed for campers, weekenders and tourists. The food was expensive, it was difficult to borrow their phone and they asked us if the place filled up to leave, even though I ordered a pretzel, soda, a veggie burger, fries, and a second soda. I was sitting in the booth looking at my guidebook when I realized I had been on the trail and the journey for 85 days.

In Harpers Ferry West Virginia Nomad and I spent eight consecutive zero days in town at the Knight Inn and then The Clarion Inn while visiting my family. My mother rented a van and drove down to vacation from New York, hearing her plan my aunt joined in on the visit traveling from Virginia (Because of Trail Days and timing we missed meeting earlier around her home near Waynesboro). We walked around Harpers Ferry and had our picture taken for the records at the ATC Conservancy. I introduced Lempsip and Rictic to my ma, who immediately gave them gracious hugs and offered the two a hitch to their booked stay at the Knight Inn.

In the afternoon we drove to a nearby REI gear store looking for new hiking gaiters and went to a casino with the ultimate hiker buffet. There was an ice-cream bar! With my aunt we went to flea markets, a vineyard for samples of peach sangria and hibachi for dinner. We spent another one of our zero days exploring around Harpers Ferry and heading back to the casino for seconds during Memorial Day for their barbecue buffet. The evening at the casino ended with a show, watching a table full of women stuff their purses full with potatoes from the buffet. I only wish all hikers who walked thru West Virginia were there to stuff their packs with potatoes as well.

Chapter 10: Hiker Traditions

After developing hiker hunger, never missing a buffet and acquiring a solid trail family to share with one of the consequential hiker traditions is to develop a grand story about the first time you saw a bear. If you are an avid hiker you will develop a second, third and fourth story about the several bears that can be found on the trail. If you are me, well then there is only the moose.

I hiked over a thousand miles along the Appalachian Trail and although Nomad saw a bear and we spent one night at the shelter in Virginia not far from Damascus where bears were stealing food, I saw nothing. I don't have the best of vision and I closed my eyes tightly at night to avoid the mice, but I was hoping to at least see one bear outside of a cage on the trail. (The Bear Mountain Zoo in New York is the lowest point along the Appalachian Trail and famous for it's trailside bears).

During the spring a group of hikers and I took up lodging at a place in Hampton Tennessee called the Braemar Castle Hostel. We were sitting around the kitchen table sorting through the hiker box when the talk turned to bears. The trail we were heading out for in the morning was closed to everyone but thru hikers passing around Watuga Lake. The Watuga Lake Shelter was closed down the year before from noted bear activity` and the guidebook suggested hikers to "Cook away from shelter and properly store your food" along with the eerie side thought "Not known when it will reopen".

In the morning I woke up late and set out to hike thru Tennessee bear country. As the last one to leave the hostel I hiked alone throughout the four miles of "closed trail". I was too nervous for my breakfast of poptarts and energy bloks, I only lingered at the closed shelter for a picture of the bear trap. The trail seemed otherwise at a stand still, I was skeptic about making any noise and walked nervously for miles. I wasn't the only nervous one though; a small southbound turtle startled himself at the sound of my incoming footsteps on the trail. He was in such a hurry to leave the woods that he was hiking the opposite way.

The trail narrowed as it continued on and at Watuga Dam I stopped when I heard a noise following behind me. I looked around hoping it was just the turtle, but he wasn't that fast, it turned out the sound was from two quickly passing backpackers who laughed when I suggested that they could have been two bears.

Another hiker tradition after bear stories and the traditional hike naked day (didn't happen - it was hailing and the black flies would have been terrible) is in the sharing of grand ghost stories. After passing the Watuga Dam miles later at Vandeventer Shelter I had lunch with a previous year thru hiker who suggested I keep hiking for the day and not to stay around at the shelter during the night. He shared a story that the shelter was, in his opinion, haunted and unsafe for women. It was a known legend that years earlier a young woman was murdered by a hatchet wielding mad man who was out for her pack. (Backpacking packs can become expensive, but murder does seem a little obsessive). The murderer was either a stranger, or her boyfriend, depending on the accuracy of the retelling. A few hikers who have stayed at Vandeventer shelter since have woke up in the middle of the night hearing hurried footsteps. One hiker has claimed to hear a chilling voice coming out from the depths of the woods.

Ghost story or not, the murder was real and I chose to keep hiking after the legend was passed on to me. I set my sights on a sixteen-mile day camping far away from the bears and the mysterious ghost related shelter hauntings.

My favorite haunted hiker story follows a hike along the Appalachian Trail in New York, not far from home. I was alone at the time, making trail in the newly fallen snow past the A.T Railroad Station and on the northbound route to reach the Connecticut border. I knew I was alone, because I sunk into the trail and wore microspikes to form a path in the snow, mine were the only footprints.

After hours in the hills passing the edge of farms, the trail turns into the woods for miles where the path becomes dark and narrow. As the trail continues to grow narrower there is a section walking along wooden planks with thick bushes surrounding on all sides, it was there I looked at the guidebook and realized the trail was behind the grounds of the former Wingdale Psychiatric Hospital. The asylum closed in the early nineties and at some point in time the Appalachian Trail was rerouted further away from the grounds. The original trail route for years came up near the hospital cemetery, where the vast field is covered with yards of unmarked graves.

Thinking about the graves hidden underneath the snow I held on tightly to my trekking poles and hurried my pace along the thin closed in trail. It might have been my pace or coincidence, but I found myself slipping on a small decline and when I tried to pull myself up, I realized my trekking pole was splintered jaggedly in half. Unsure what to do I used the one remaining pole for balance and held onto the sharp broken pole for safekeeping. I was passing a dark line of trees I looked up and realized a sign nailed into the wood, I couldn't make out the words but the sign was painted and chipped with dark red splinters. I stopped for a moment trying to get a closer look at the sign when I noticed the crows flying overhead. At that moment I remembered the story behind the graves, that before the trail was rerouted, before the asylum came to be, the buildings were used as a prison. Beside the idea of ghosts, I thought of how in the facilities history, several convicts escaped to the same woods I stood in. I looked around anxiously and saw one more sign on a tree ahead on the trail. There above the white trail blaze was a warning "This area is under surveillance". That was enough for me; I booked the rest of the New York miles so fast I didn't stop again until I reached the Connecticut border.

My pace into Connecticut and later miles past the border towards the town of Kent did lead to another unplanned hiker tradition, in a trip to urgent care.

Traditionally long distance hikers are known to break a leg, wear down their feet or improperly fall ill from unfiltered stream water leading to a necessary side trip to urgent care. I didn't break any bones, but I was weary from hiking around the grounds of the former asylum. Not wanting to hear any more ghost stories I hiked from the New York Connecticut border, eleven miles, passing the Ten Mile River Shelter and Bulls Bridge. I met a sincere group of flip floppers who started at Harpers Ferry, they were return hikers with the trail calling them back every year, they set out to hike again. After stopping for lunch and wishing them luck I spent the afternoon following the blazes looking at the fire damage of the land around me. After Mt Algo Shelter, a feeling about the trail brought me to bushwhack down a hill.

Bushwhacking in Connecticut, the state most known for lyme disease, is never a great idea. I thought I was lucky when I reached a road and looked down, at a glance there was only mud and dirt covering my legs.

Unable to find a hitch, possibly because of my clothing and the leaves in my hair, I walked for miles along roads before meeting two other hikers heading out of town. The two men were looking for a hitch back to the trail and I shrugged, I thought it was hard walking to find the town, never considering getting back to the trail. The hikers nodded from across the street and suggested I head over to Backcountry Outfitters for the best meal. I headed up the street, brushed the remaining leaves out of my hair the best I could and sat my pack down outside the building.

I was relaxing in the outfitters, having lost most of my trail lunch earlier due to the flies, and was enjoying the food when I noticed the napkins on the windowsill. At my table in-between spoonful's of mixed berry sorbet I carefully uncovered some of the dirt from my left leg. I wasn't sure why some of the dirt seemed dark and immovable until I realized it wasn't all dirt, I had countless ticks settling in around my knee. After incorrectly attempting to remove half of a tick from my leg I was later reasoned to stop in for a visit to urgent care.

Because I had lyme disease twice before and upon hearing I was hiking in the woods of Connecticut with the intention of leaving soon for Maine, I returned from the doctor with copious amounts of sunscreen and medication for lyme disease. Although the medicine works wonders, it has a common side effect of burning the skin when exposed to sunlight. As a fair skinned, freckled red head I burn normally without having lyme disease. I was set back a few days from hiking, another hiker tradition, and spent my time looking for a new trekking umbrella to keep out the sun and a new pair of gloves to cover my hands. Having the hiker luck of another setback I waited until I was ready and slowly counted down the days until I could head out and return to the trail.

When I did return to the trail and headed the way from Maine it was there that I found the moose. Three moose's to be accurate, if counting is essential to the tradition. The first moose was a stuffed animal bear and he was bought in Millinocket Maine, taken down from a store side room shelf, named Moose and strapped to the back of my pack as some form of irony. Hikers traditionally carry unnecessary weight and Moose was an attempt at winning the luxury item contest among hikers. Along the trail there were a fair number of hikers carrying pillows, books, small ironic figurines to pose for pictures, flasks of whiskey and even in extreme cases, soap.

Chapter 11: Katahdin

In June Nomad and I rented a car and drove six hours north of New York to Bangor Maine. We stopped once we reached the Maine border, him for lobster, and I for Vermont grilled cheese. We sat for an hour adding on a buffet and watching the sway of the lobsters in the water. In Bangor since we arrived late, Nomad bribed the local bus driver with a Snapple bottle and five dollars to hold the bus, while I dropped off our rental car at the airport across the street. I drove for the first time in months, realizing that although I preferred my feet, it was amusing to be behind the wheel again, my vision seemed stronger. After running around the airport looking for the key drop off location, I sprinted back to the bus and then we were on our way to Millinocket, the gateway town to the northern terminus of the Appalachian Trail.

The bus dropped us off at a gas station one town away in Medway, where we unloaded our packs along with a new southbound hiker while we waited for a ride. Curiously an hour later, we learned from locals that there was a bad storm and the entire town of Millinocket lost power. Our shuttle ride had no electricity to call and we failed to find a hitch without southern hospitality, after being eaten by the black flies we called around until we found an expensive shuttle into town.

In Millinocket there were trees and branches down on every road of the dark unlit town. Our shuttle dropped us off at the hiker lodge in the pitch dark.

Nomad and I tried to find our way around the building with our headlamps and struggled until we heard hikers voices coming from a nearby common room. We stayed up that night eating pizza by candlelight and sharing stories with a hiker from the Bronx. He recently left the trail ill and came back from the hospital with a diagnosis of overhydration. Weary and exhausted, Nomad and I took the advice to rest up and planned on a zero day in the morning.

Millinocket was lovely even without the southern hospitality; we had breakfast in town at the Appalachian Trail Café, sat in the square for ice cream and met a new hiker named Stepping Wolf along with his dog Maggie. We received the best advice at the lodge when we were advised about the earlier black flies and went out to purchase bug netting for our heads. Unaware to us, Maine was settling in black fly season and every hiker was advised on spray, netting and keeping a fast pace while on the trail. If the pace was too slow or if we took to long a break, the flies would descend in swarms.

In the morning we woke up early and headed out with four other hikers from the lodge in a shuttle to Baxter State Park. Everyone in the van seemed nervous as the road took us closer to the mountains and Katahdin loomed overhead. One by one we registered at the ranger's station and I was given the number as the 230 person to attempt to summit Katahdin that year (I was number 303 when starting at Springer Mountain back in Georgia). The ranger asked if we were northbounders, southbounders or starting in

Maine as flip-flop hikers. We were labeled as flip flop hikers, hikers who don't keep to the traditional trail route. Nomad and I hiked north from the traditional start of the trail in Georgia to West Virginia, I hiked portions of New York and Connecticut, and then we flip flopped to Maine. As flip floppers, Nomad and I switched into daypacks for the climb up Katahdin and left the rest of our gear temporarily behind on the ranger's porch with the others. We waved to our shuttle driver and wished the new hikers, who were about to take their first trail steps, good luck. In response we learned that the young man we drove along with was indeed planning to make every mile and hike the entire way southbound wearing a large sombrero on his head.

In Baxter State Park Nomad and I were glad to see the white blazes again and start our final stretch heading north to Katahdin. We hiked a few miles north and stopped at the falls before heading up the increasing incline steep boulder fields. Along the way we met another flip flopper who hiked to the rebar, the metal rung put into the rocks for support, on the mountain and had to turn back without summiting. He said it was "too windy and unsafe for a solo hiker". We also met a woman hiking down who warned about a group of "inexperienced hikers" who were turning around and had "no right to be up on the mountain." Hearing this, I took a break to add on my leggings underneath my shorts; I already tripped, felt the pain of one bloody knee and awhile left to go before the summit. Above the tree line I discovered how gorgeous Maine could be and also how dangerous. The winds were strong and the rocks were a scramble aside jagged cliffs. I lost count of the number of times Nomad held onto me or hoisted me up over a large grouping of rocks. We were climbing, me literally crawling and holding onto the mountain's rocks as balance, for hours.

We were the last hikers of the day to reach the summit. Mt. Katahdin. The final white blaze of the Appalachian Trail. After hiking two miles above tree line and several false summits we reached the final sign and we had it all to ourselves. Normally Katahdin's summit is crowded with day hikers, giving a moment alone to a backpacker, impossible. Together we read the sign Katahdin, Baxter Peak, Elevation 5,267 FT. Around 2,190 miles of trail spread out from where we stood, to our first white blaze back in Georgia, we hiked over a thousand miles to get there. With an hour left until sundown Nomad and I stood before the end of the trail in awe. I wanted to cry, instead I kissed Nomad and then I kissed the sign. In the cold and wind we clung onto each other looking out at the mountains stretched beyond us.

With the sunlight fading we took one last look around us and headed south back down the mountain. We were at the rocks climbing down from the boulder fields when the sky turned to dark. Since we switched out for daypacks earlier, we didn't have all of our gear, a tent, or the light of our headlamps. Nomad and I were hiking down Mt. Katahdin with only the pale light of the moon to guide us back. From the moonlight, we could barely follow the trail, searching desperately for the next white blaze to lead us away from the cliffs.

When we descended below the tree line, away from the rocks, it was warmer away from the wind, but it was also darker and harder to see in the forest. Nomad held my phone up behind me as I lead the way following the blazes under its feeble light. We continued to lose the trail around turns, fall and I tripped on several rocks that were too dark to see. At one point I fell down so far Nomad wasn't sure I was going to stand back up again. After a break to steady my tired legs, we hiked on into the night for hours, only stopping when we spotted a large set of animal eyes glowing from beyond the shadow of the trees.

Hours and hours later after thinking we heard the motions of running water we rejoiced at the sounds of the Katahdin Stream Falls. After the falls the trail began to level off and we realized we were almost down from the mountain. I stumbled one last time on a rock in the trail and then hurried my pace on the level ground heading us back to the campground. Back at the trailhead, I opened the logbook we signed in the morning and checked us back down safe and sound, marking the time two in the morning. We hiked for sixteen hours trekking the 10.4 miles round trip of Mount Katahdin, we were beyond exhausted, but we made it.

All was quiet in Baxter State Park, since we were the last one's to summit everyone else was asleep in their tents or Lean-to's. We were back at the camp long past hiker midnight; even the weekend campers were asleep. At the ranger station no ranger was around to offer guidance or assign a tent spot, we opened the door to the porch and looked in the dark for the only two packs left behind. Thankful for our packs and headlamps we sorted our equipment, returned our borrowed day packs to their bin and walked until we found an unused lean-to labeled campsite ten. With our legs barely functioning after sixteen hours of hiking we crawled into our sleeping bags and fell immediately asleep.

In the morning the first thing I saw when I opened my eyes were my hiking shorts hanging on the peg on the wall, they were covered in large holes. I knew I fell beyond a reasonable amount on the hike, but I didn't realize in the dark, how serious the falls were. If I hadn't stopped as I did to add on another layer with my leggings I may not have made it, those shorts literally saved my ass.

HIKER GLOSSARY

A.T.

The Appalachian Trail is a footpath for travelers which span's the eastern coast of the United States from Georgia to Maine. The length of the trail changes from rerouting and is currently over 2,000 miles long. The trail passes along towns, roads, bridges, mountains and the wilderness.

Aqua Blaze

When a person travels along the water, away from the white blazes often on a boat or raft to make for quicker miles. Not for purists.

Base Weight

The mass of a hikers pack without food or water accounted for. Can be under 10lbs to 82 or more.

Bear Bag

A bag used to store hiker's food. The bag is durable and weighed heavily with anywhere from a day to a weeks worth of sustenance.

Bear Box

A sealed box used to store bear bags. Proofed for protection.

Bear Cables

Often found at shelters in bear sighted areas. A system of cables used to hoist bear bags into the air at high tree branch level, away from the capable grasp of bears.

Benton MacKaye Trail

Known fondly as the BMT, a nearly three hundred-mile path in the Appalachian Mountains.

Blue Blaze

A blue painted mark often found on rocks or trees announcing a side trail along the Appalachian Trail. Frequently leads hikers to side trails, vistas and parking lots.

Brown Blazing

Hiking following along privies on and off the trail.

Bushwhacking

Leaving marked trail and travelling into highly dense bushes, thickets and forest.

Cowboy Camp

Sleeping underneath the stars without a tent (hopefully on a warm night).

Creeper Trail

A thirty-five mile trail that follows and crosses along the Appalachian Trail. A destination for day hikers, bikers and Virginian locals.

Flip-Flopping

When a hiker travels in a non-traditional route, often to avoid overcrowding or weather conditions. Example: travelling north from Georgia to West Virginia, then jumping to another section of the trail and traveling southbound.

Gaiters

Outerwear for the feet, serves as protection against mud and rain on the trail.

Harpers Ferry

The hikers psychological half waypoint on the Appalachian Trail, located in West Virginia along the ATC National Headquarters.

Hiker Box

Often left in hostels, trailside motels and stores to contain left behind or trade hiker items. A hiker can drop in surplus food or supplies and take items that they need.

Hiker Hunger

Consuming vast amounts of calories as a necessity for burning calories at a rapid pace while hiking long miles. Frequently bushwhacking into town for a buffet meal or the promise of consuming an entire extra large pizza.

Hostel

A welcoming destination for travelers to spend the night, shower, resupply and consume a warm meal.

HYOH

Hike your own hike. Enjoy your own journey. Don't be rude. Respect the trail and it's people.

Katahdin

A strategically difficult mountain to climb with ascents above tree line requiring the hiker to use rebars. The mountain is home to the northern terminus and final northbound blaze on the trail.

L.N.T

Leave no trace principles, general ideas set down for hikers to maintain trail longevity. Take only memories, respect the trail along with wildlife, minimize impacts and be considerate.

Lasher

Long ass section hiker. Typically five hundred miles or more in one time frame.

Logbook

A journal found in shelters, left behind with pen or pencil for hikers to sign with their thoughts, advice, daily miles, and messages to other hikers. Notorious for soaking wet, misplacement, theft and enjoyable reading material when found.

Lyme Disease

A disease passed from deer ticks that latch onto hikers. It can lead to countless ailments, deficiency's complications and even death.

Mail Drop

A package sent to a hiker along the trail, containing food and supplies from home.

Microspikes

Footgear placed around and underneath hiking shoes to clamp to snow along with ice on the trail.

Nero Day

Hiking near zero miles, strategically planning miles to end up in town for restaurants and resupply.

NoBo

Northbound hiker.

One Hundred Mile Wilderness

A remote area of the trail located in Maine that does not intersect with towns. Miles upon miles of seclusion, moose and root covered paths.

Privy

A bathroom found along the trail near shelters, consisting of walls and a roof above a non-traditional toilet. Some have no doors, some are pit holes and others are simply wonderful escapes to do ones business in privacy.

PUDS

Pointless ups and downs along the trail.

Purist

Hiking every white blaze on the trail, every mile without skipping, slackpacking or rerouting.

Rebar

Steel reinforcing bars that trail maintenance workers inserted into rocks, they are necessary for traversing difficult terrain. A hikers holds onto the rebar while obtaining footing to hoist themselves over bouldering fields or outcroppings.

Section Hiker

Hiking a section or segment, one state on the trail or one stretch for weeks.

Shelter

A building with three walls and a roof located near a water source on the trail. Typical shelters can hold anywhere from 6-10 hikers sleeping on the floor for a nights stay.

Shuttle

Transportation provided occasionally for free and other times at a set fee for hikers in a large vehicle, van or bus. Travel to town from the trail or from a town back to the trail.

Skipping

Bypassing trail miles, mountains or sections of white blazed A.T. markers.

Slackpacking

Switching out a full gear pack for a day bag. Travelling long miles quicker and lighter.

SoBo

Southbound hiker.

Soloing

Traveling alone on the trail. Hiking at ones own pace, with only themself for company.

Springer

The southern terminus of the Appalachian Trail. The mountain containing the first white blaze for northbound hikers. The location of a logbook to sign at the peaks summit stored inside a rock.

Stealth Camp

Setting up a tent off the trail and away from trail shelters. Tenting in unmarked fields or small flat areas a distance from water sources and the path.

The Smokies

The Great Smoky National Park. The range of trail that travels along the Tennessee and North Carolina Mountains. The area is well known for Clingman's Dome the highest elevation on the trail, wilderness, regulations, large stone shelters and the complete and total absence of privies.

The Virginia Blues

Feelings of depression or monotony a hiker finds while traveling the 554 miles along the states farms, towns, puds and mountains.

Trail Angel

A person who provides assistance to hikers, in food, rides to/from town, a place to stay, necessary items, conversation and encouragement.

Trail Days

A festival held annually in the trail town of Damascus Virginia. The largest gathering within the hiker community, containing venders, music, contests, gear shops, presentations and a hiker parade.

Thru Hiker

Hiking the entire trail in one year's time.

Trail Magic

Food or drink provided for hikers. In addition: medical supplies and necessities.

Trail Name

A nickname that is associated with the hiking community.

Trail Town

A town located close to the trail. A location of resupply or hiker zero days supplied with a post office, grocery store, hostel and restaurants.

Tramily

Trail Family. The people a hiker chooses to surround themselves with, for support and companionship.

Trek

Travelling along, setting the pace of a backpackers journey.

Ultralight

Hiking using extremely lightweight gear, practicing the method of counting ounces and shaving off unnecessary pack heaviness.

White Blaze

The official markers of the Appalachian Trail painted white and found on rocks, trees, bridges and along the hikers path.

Yellow Blazing

Hitching rides around sections of the trail, instead of hiking every white blaze.

Zero Day

Hiking zero traditional trail miles, staying in town to resupply food, recover and relax.

ABOUT THE AUTHOR

Graduated from Sarah Lawrence College in New York the author Lisa Cohen is an avid writer, hiker and activist for brain injury awareness. Raven is her second published book after her recovery memoir Walnut; she plans to continue sharing stories along her journey.

Resources

American Brain Tumor Association
8550 W. Bryn Mawr Ave. Ste 550
Chicago, IL 60631

Appalachian Trail Conservancy
799 Washington Street PO Box 807
Harpers Ferry, WV 25425-0807

Brain Injury Association of America
1608 Spring Hill Road Suite 110
Vienna, VA 22182

National Brain Tumor Society
55 Chapel St. Suite 200
Newton, MA 02458